CONTENTS

CASE STUDIES

IMI
BEST PRACTICE
HR IN IRELAND

John Cullen
Martin Farrelly

in association with

www.oaktreepress.com

OAK TREE PRESS
19 Rutland Street, Cork, Ireland
www.oaktreepress.com

A catalogue record of this book is
available from the British Library.

ISBN 1-904887-01-5

Printed in Ireland by ColourBooks.

EDITORS

JOHN CULLEN is Senior Management Researcher at IMI's Centre for Management Research. He has published in several academic and practitioner journals in Ireland, the US and the UK. His research interests include organisational and management learning, competitiveness, strategic intelligence and management labour markets. He has Master's degrees from NUI Maynooth and University College Dublin and is currently completing doctoral research on management learning and organisational cultures at Lancaster University Management School.

MARTIN FARRELLY is Human Resource Management specialist at IMI and is responsible for the design and delivery of all HR programmes. Prior to joining IMI, Martin gained extensive experience in the HR function in the services, financial services, telecommunications and food manufacturing sectors. He holds the National Diploma in Personnel Management, a Master's degree in Organisational Behaviour, is a Chartered Fellow of CIPD and has completed the Human Resource Executive programme at the University of Michigan.

CONTRIBUTORS

HR Department – Abbott Ireland

Grace Perrott – Head of Employee Research, AIB Group

Catherine Whelan – Programme Manager, AXA Ireland

Patricia Normanly – Equality & Diversity Officer, Dublin Bus

Patrick Garvey – Secretary / PRO, Flour Confectioners & Bakers Association

Alistair McMenamin – Hibernian Life & Pensions

David Webster – General Manager, Hilton Dublin Airport

Kevin McNamara – HR Manager, HP Ireland

Mary O'Connor – Human Resources Manager, KARE

Sonya Mahood – Recruitment Manager for Ireland, Oracle Ireland

Martin Bourke – Head of Corporate Affairs, Public Appointments Service

Louise Barrett – Former HR Officer, Trócaire

DEDICATION

For
Fiona and Adam
&
Eithne, Jane, Rory, Alice and Liam.

Thank you for your love and support.

Acknowledgements

We wish to thank IMI Chief Executive, Dr. Tom McCarthy, and CIPD Director, Mr. Michael McDonnell, for their help and support in the completion of this book. We also wish to thank Mr. Frank Brennan at CIPD, Kevin Spring and Kevin Empey at Watson Wyatt, and Dr. John Mangan and Marion O'Connor at IMI, for their assistance in assembling the book, which proved critical throughout the project.

A special note of thanks is extended to all of the managers who contributed the cases and agreed to allow their work to be used as examples of best practice.

Finally, we wish to thank Brian O'Kane and the staff of Oak Tree Press for all their encouragement and support.

1
INTRODUCTION

Assembling a book about best practices in human resource management in the Irish context is very much like trying to hit several moving targets at once. Each of the three identifiable themes in our title appear to be facing pivotal moments of rupture, change and re-definition. What exactly is the Irish context? What is happening to management? What is the point in assembling a book on Best Practice when the world of work and organisations changes so rapidly?

The change in our national economic fortunes has been very well-documented. Since 1995, Ireland has undergone a decade of sustained economic growth, with the result that it now enjoys higher numbers in employment than at any time in its history. The economic boom of the late 1990s resulted in the 'Celtic Tiger' economy that saw the reversal of long-established Irish emigration trends, reductions in Government debt as a percentage of GNP, lowering of corporate and personal taxation rates and improvements in both GDP and GNP *per capita*. This boom was largely facilitated by policies, many of which date back to the late 1950s, that abandoned protectionism, encouraged foreign direct investment, and advocated membership of the EC and greater investment in education (MacSharry & White, 2001).

The global economic downturn in 2001 brought to light several negative effects of the 'boom' era. Although standards of living have increased, Ireland has become a very expensive economy in which to live and do business. By January 2003, Ireland's rate of inflation was twice the EU average and the rate of price increases had risen to three and a half times that of the UK (Ireland's main

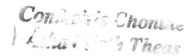

trading partner). Considerable threats have arisen to Ireland's competitive position with regard to attracting and retaining foreign direct investment. The substantial increase in the Irish cost base has occurred almost simultaneously with the accession of 10 new member states to the EU, all of which currently have lower cost-bases, young educated populations and will be the preferred recipients for aid for enterprise. On a global level, economies such as China and India also offer low costs and enormous supplies of skilled labour.

As a small open economy, Ireland is highly vulnerable to changes in the global competitive demography. With a view to addressing this, the Tánaiste and Minister for Enterprise, Trade & Employment recently convened a high-level consultative group (The Enterprise Strategy Group) to advise on enterprise policy and strategy. This Group reported in July 2004 and proposed a model that identified five sources of competitive advantage for Ireland:

- Expertise in markets
- Expertise in technology – product & service development
- World-class skills, education & training
- An attractive taxation regime
- Effective, agile government.

Four conditions were identified as being essential to drive these sources of competitive advantage:

- Cost competitiveness
- Physical and communications infrastructure
- Innovation and entrepreneurship
- Management capability.

Bearing these conditions and desired advantages in mind, it is important to remember that the demographic profile of Ireland is radically changing and that Irish identity is undergoing a re-adjustment at a fundamental level. It is not just that we are no longer a mono-cultural country; we are a society that is increasingly dependent on new non-Irish populations to meet our labour force needs.

When 'personnel' management became 'human resource' management, it was to a large extent a recognition of the fact that, without people, an organisation is effectively a soulless entity. Human resource management is an acknowledgement that a key (perhaps *the* key) component of any managerial scenario is that individual human beings, with their skills, attributes and complex needs are crucial to making any strategic initiative happen.

> 'People are the only element with the inherent power to generate value. All other variables offer nothing but inert potential. By their nature, they add nothing, and they cannot add anything until some human being leverages that potential by putting it into play.'
> (Jac Fitz-Ens, 2000)

For any person to be treated like any other material resource available to a corporate entity is intolerable. It is true that organisations exist to meet stated aims: to make profit, to provide a service, to meet a social need. We may work because we have to pay our way in the world but, in a full-employment society, we have choices to do this in ways that meet higher-level needs such as helping society cure itself from its ills. Jean-Paul Sartre wrote that people read books to give meaning to their lives. It is possibly truer to say that people work to give meaning to their own lives and to enrich the lives of their families and communities. If an organisation impedes how an individual can do this, that organisation very quickly will find itself with difficulties in recruiting and retaining the very people who can help it meet its aims.

Following the high-profile corporate scandals of the first years of the new millennium, theorists focused on issues such as Corporate Governance and Corporate Social Responsibility in response to the battering that the image of management had taken during these years. More recently, there has been a more fundamental questioning of what it is that the discipline of management seeks to be. One of the very last papers (published posthumously in *Academy of Management Learning & Education*) by one of the most influential organisational theorists of recent times, Sumantra Ghoshal, articulates discomfort with the way in which the ideology of management education is oriented towards profit maximisation rather than in the direction of recognising the huge possibilities that organisational life can bring to employees, managers and society in general. There is a tangible growth in the number of articles and texts being produced that seek to understand organisations as creators of meaning rather than as engines of profit-generation and nothing else. Stories, narratives, conversations and language in organisational settings are being treated as legitimate sources of data for research because, in essence, they make up how individuals understand the considerable proportions of their lives that they spend in organisations.

HR managers find themselves at the nodal point in the organisation where economic trends, productivity capability and human lives overlap. They stand at the intersect of the organisation's culture, structure and strategy, and deal with issues as they present from all angles. At the time of writing this *Introduction*, positive growth predictions for the Irish economy over 2005 anticipated the need for greater levels of recruitment. During the height of the Celtic Tiger years, high demand for employees resulted in significant tension in the Irish labour market and it appears that demands for talented employees are beginning to increase again. Once again, the ability to create a culture where employees are valued and developed according to their and the organisation's needs, and where key talent is identified, recruited and retained, is critical to achieving success.

This book is not a 'how-to' guide written from a detached academic perspective. It aims to provide a set of 'real world' examples where organisations addressed a need generated by the rapid pace of change in Irish society, and rose to meet the challenge. It looks at 12 specific cases under the headings of:

- **Culture:** AIB Group / Hibernian Life & Pensions / HP Ireland
- **Recruitment & Retention:** Oracle Ireland / Hilton Group
- **Organisational Learning:** Flour Confectioners & Bakers Association / Abbott Ireland
- **Work / Life balance:** Trócaire / KARE
- **Diversity:** Dublin Bus
- **Innovation:** AXA Ireland / Public Appointments Service.

These case examples represent inputs from MNC subsidiaries, large Irish organisations, the public sector and not-for-profit organisations, working in sectors as diverse as financial services, transport, technology and overseas development. HR managers and departments are continually faced with having to come up rapidly with solutions to complex social and cultural issues. *Best Practice HR in Ireland* aims to showcase some of the responses that HR managers and departments have adopted to address issues which their organisations faced. The managers and their organisations have been most generous in sharing these with us, to produce a collection of learnings that can be used in a practical sense by managers in different settings.

References

Enterprise Strategy Group (2004). *Ahead of the Curve: Ireland's Place in the Global Economy*, Dublin: Forfás.

Fitz-Ens, J. (2000). *The ROI of Human Capital*, New York, AMACOM.

Ghoshal, S. (2005). 'Bad Management Theories are Destroying Good Management Practices', *Academy of Management Learning & Education*, 4(1), pp.75-91.

MacSharry, R. & White, P. (2000). *The Making of the Celtic Tiger: The Inside Story of Ireland's Boom Economy*, Dublin: Mercier Press.

2

CULTURE

Culture is one of the most enduring concepts in organisation theory and human resource practice. One of the key reasons for the continuing fascination with culture amongst managers and academics is perhaps due to the tacit acknowledgement that it somehow holds the key to organisational success through the very people who work in these organisations.

It is impossible to imagine discussions of topics such as leadership and performance without reference to culture. Corporate culture had been a topic of academic study since the first half of the 20th century, but it was not until the early 1980s that it underwent something of a boom. Since then, it has remained a subject of critical interest to managers in all settings.

The fact that thousands of definitions exist does not help to clarify the often vague and nebulous concept of culture, but perhaps serves best to underscore that it is both highly complex and important, needing detailed attention from scholars, and clarification by managers.

Some of the bestselling business books of all time, such as Charles Handy's *Understanding Organisations*, Peters & Waterman's hugely influential *In Search of Excellence* and Deal & Kennedy's *Corporate Culture*, communicate the importance of understanding organisational culture as the key element in developing high-performing organisations. Since then, the study of organisational culture has led to heated debate (described by some of the leading scholars in the organisational culture field as an 'unholy war') which, again, perhaps is indicative of just how vital culture is to the survival of organisations. A very rudimentary description of this debate centres on the issue of whether culture is something that can be managed, controlled and changed objectively, or whether culture is something that just is, open to various multiple interpretations by any number of actors in a single organisational setting, and which changes of its own volition. Both viewpoints are probably true to varying extents, but the main benefit to managers arising from the 'unholy war' is that a variety of tools have emerged that aid understanding and developing culture.

One of the most celebrated writers on organisational culture working today, Professor Mats Alvesson, describes culture as 'a tricky concept as it is easily used to cover everything and consequently nothing'. An example of just how tricky culture can be is often demonstrated by media reports of organisational failure or misbehaviour where senior executives are chastised for failing to address how certain cultural practices had emerged in their businesses. Glance through recent newspaper business sections or corporate websites and it becomes evident that organisations routinely use the term 'culture' to underscore what it is about the people in their organisations that they wish to promote: 'a can-do culture'; 'a fast-paced and flexible culture'; 'a dynamic and customer-focused culture'; 'a strong culture of compliance' – the descriptions abound. Yet, unfortunately the term 'culture' is often levied at organisations in court cases involving employee mistreatment, bullying and harassment.

It is perhaps most useful to think of culture in terms of not only 'how things are done around here', as cited by Deal & Kennedy (1982), but also as 'how things are not done around here'. Culture can prove a very real impediment to getting things done in organisations, and sometimes even to making sure that the right thing is not done. In some cases, it can prove pathological to the organisation itself. One of the strongest examples of this was provided by Diane Vaughan in *The Challenger Launch Decision*, where it was demonstrated how cultural belief systems ultimately contributed to a decision by NASA to issue an unsafe shuttle launch decision – with tragic consequences.

A central concept that emerged from the corporate culture gurus of the 1980s was the notion of organisations having cultures, which could variously be described as weak or strong. Strong cultures were those where the commitment of all employees to the same set of cultural values would result in higher levels of organisational performance. Several writers have contended that perspectives on organisational culture exist at organisational, departmental / functional and individual levels (Stanford Graduate Business School Professor Joanne Martin named these integrated, differentiated and fragmented cultural perspectives). In his history of the Kerry Group, James J. Kennelly writes of a corporate culture forged at a time when considerable obstacles that threatened to prevent its advancement were overcome by strong resolve, hard work and a sense of refusing to fail. Although this culture was not planned or written down, it emerged as one of the key drivers of one of Ireland's most successful multinational companies.

Ireland has punched well above its weight in terms of its creativity on the international stage. We have produced some of the most outstanding artistic innovators in the creative arts in the world over the last 100 or so years. The culture of the country during the earlier years of the 20th century, however, forced writers, such as Joyce and Beckett, to leave Ireland for countries where their innovations would receive better welcomes than they had experienced at home.

Irish society has undergone fundamental change since then, and it is now a stated priority for the ongoing health of the economy that we move up the value chain in terms of innovation. It is crucial, therefore, that organisations encourage the development of organisational cultures where innovation can be recognised, exploited and made part of the fabric of daily life in Irish business. Companies such as 3M emphasise innovation as a cornerstone of their culture; innovation is emphasised as a value throughout the organisation. We know from international studies of business cultures that Irish people are individualistic, comfortable with risk, and egalitarian in our management style (for a summary of these studies of Irish business cultures, see Cullen, 2004). When these attributes are coupled with a tradition of creativity, the enormous potential for innovation in Ireland is visible. The lesson is that we have the capability and desire to be innovative. We need to ensure that this happens, by encouraging cultures of innovation in our organisations.

Culture is not a vague concept; it is a highly complex and multi-dimensional one. It is crucial that culture be explored, in order to ensure that it encourages performance and innovation, rather than bureaucracy and stagnation.

Because culture is created and experienced by groups of people, HR functions have a major role in ensuring that the culture of organisations are reflective of business needs. Employees are the most important source of capital in organisations and a committed and motivated staff is the central component that drives organisations forward and ensures competitiveness. As other nations increasingly offer similar, and in some cases, better, incentives than Ireland to global firms to move their activities to their locations, our people, their creativity and productivity will be central to sustaining our attractiveness as a nation. The role of organisational culture in innovation is thus fundamental.

In something of a clarion call for the creation of work cultures that are generative of innovation, Charles Leadbeater (2003) has written:

> 'It has long been recognized that innovation is a social process, in which ideas are developed collaboratively through networks and face-to-face interaction. The more uncertain and fuzzy the innovation, the more likely it is that it will develop through intensive collaboration in networks and clusters of the kind that Silicon Valley exemplifies. People invariably need to meet, face-to-face, to explore and resolve complex problems, especially when innovation is at its earliest, fuzziest states when its outcome and direction are most

uncertain. Creativity is possible only if people are willing to expose themselves by revealing untried and untested ideas. Encouraging people to take that risk is difficult unless they feel trusted. Trust is a vital lubricant of innovation because it encourages risk-taking, and trust thrives amid networks of collaboration.'

HR cultural initiatives have dual goals: understanding the culture of organisation and how it is perceived by those who are members of the organisation, and shaping the culture of the organisation in a way that meets the needs of clients and the market.

The three cases that follow discuss some very different cultural initiatives, showing how two large Irish organisations, and one multinational, approached the issues of understanding and aligning their cultures. The first reports the work of AIB Group's Employee Research Unit in developing a *People Focus Index*, which represents a real attempt to understand employee commitment and to align it with the organisation's goals of customer satisfaction and financial performance. The second reports on two initiatives that ran concurrently in Hibernian Life & Pensions, which attempted to align three different corporate cultures and address the needs of customers and clients of the organisation. The final case in this chapter discusses HP Ireland's use of the *Balanced Scorecard* technique to manage knowledge and human capital in a large and complex setting.

References

Alvesson, M. (2002). *Understanding Organisational Culture*, London, Sage.

Cullen, J. (2004). 'Identifying Sectoral Management Cultures through Recruitment Advertising', *The Leadership & Organisation Development Journal*, 25(3), pp.279-291.

Deal, T.E. & Kennedy, A.A. (1982). *Corporate Culture,* Reading, Addison-Wesley.

Handy, C. (1999). *Understanding Organisations,* London, Penguin.

Kennelly, J.J. (2001). *The Kerry Way: The History of the Kerry Group 1972 – 2000,* Dublin: Oak Tree Press.

Leadbeater, C. (2003).*Up the Down Escalator: Why the Global Pessimists are Wrong,* London: Penguin Books.

Martin, J. (1992). *The Culture of Organisations: Three Perspectives,* New York: Oxford University Press.

Peters, T.J. & Waterman, R.H. (1982), *In Search of Excellence,* New York: Harper & Row.

Vaughan, D. (1996). *The Challenger Launch Decision: Risky Technology, Culture and Deviance at NASA,* Chicago: University of Chicago Press.

CASE 1:

The Staff Survey in AIB:
Influencing the People Management Agenda[1]

It has become increasingly recognised that staff, as key stakeholders in companies, have both the right and the responsibility to air their views on working life in a safe and confidential manner. Additionally, businesses increasingly see the need to use staff insights on both internal and external aspects of the business more effectively as a rich vein of internal and external market intelligence. Generally, it is accepted that carefully-designed staff surveys are a good tool to address these twin requirements.

Background

AIB has been surveying staff regularly since 1989. In 1997, as a result of a major review of HR, the staff survey was redesigned to provide a more robust qualitative and quantitative measurement system for the business. This survey not only provides management with insights into the views of one of the most important stakeholders, but is fully integrated into the People Management agenda – informing HR strategy, processes and practices.

As in most companies, the survey examines the 'classic' aspects of working life – for example:

- Views of performance management
- Reward
- Leadership

---

[1]   This case study was prepared with the assistance of Grace Perrott, Head of Employee Research at AIB Group.

- Alignment with strategy, etc.

Up to 2005, the survey has taken place annually and all staff are invited to take part. Typically, over 80% of staff use this opportunity to have their views heard. The survey findings are not only reported at individual team level, but also right up the organisation, up to and including Board level. Key findings are published each year in the *Group Annual Report*.

The survey is used to inform the business on broad strategic issues. In the last five years, it has been the key source of information, and in some cases the catalyst, for some important enterprise-wide changes including:

- An extensive evaluation and review of training
- The redesign and repositioning of the Performance Management system
- A review of the pay scales for more junior staff in the organisation
- The expansion of the staff consultative process.

Becoming more locally relevant

Increasingly important, the survey is used locally to inform annual business planning and review processes. This local intelligence provides excellent team-specific insights to management teams, indicating where changes or improvements may be required in any number of aspects such as operational training, management development needs, or communication gaps.

The staff survey was revised in 2000 when, for the first time, individual teams (of at least 15 staff) received survey reports. This enabled effective prioritisation and action planning to take place at local level (for example, in branches). The ability to identify and address individual team issues has been a catalyst for improvements throughout the business, and provides HR and line management with information that enables them to target specific action and support.

Until the introduction of these individual team reports, there was no objective measure available of the effectiveness of line management as 'people managers'. As the improvement and sustainment of People Management skills is a core aspect of the Group HR strategy, this had been identified as a fundamental gap.

Measuring People Management skills

Accordingly in 2001, AIB developed a *People Focus Index* (PFI), which is a key output of the survey for all teams. This is a local management index, which assesses the impact on staff of local management attitudes, skills, practices, and behaviours. The PFI was developed internally by Group Employee Research, who, with the HR Business Partners and the Management Development function, reviewed the managerial competencies identified under the People Management aspect of the line manager role. Questions were devised, with ISR, the survey supplier, to assess the impact of line management on their staff under each of these competencies.

These questions have been tested and changed, based both on statistical analysis and on changing priorities in the set of competencies identified for managers.

In 2002, the PFI was linked to the performance review process for management. In addition, extensive work was done on the identification and sharing of best practice in People Management.

Objectives of the PFI

The specific objectives of the PFI include:

- To inform the People Management improvement programme, through tracking of trends and identification of gaps in managerial competencies overall within the organisation
- To enable identification and sharing of best practices in People Management

- To provide a robust indicator of local management skills and behaviours and their impact on staff, and thus drive remedial action and support for line management
- To provide a quantitative measure to feed into the performance management process and managerial bonus allocations
- To benchmark these aspects against peer companies in the global financial services sector and against global high performing companies.

PFI – Measuring its Impact

The PFI has provided, for the first time, a key hard measure of the people-focus aspect of the job role of managers for use in performance management and reward decisions. Trend analysis shows that this has strongly influenced the way people are managed in AIB.

The PFI provides HR and line management with information enabling them to:

- Reward effective behaviours and deter ineffective behaviours
- Target remedial work
- Provide support to management and teams, where appropriate.

The PFI enables the business to identify and share best practice within the company and, each year, a best practice guide is updated and published based on these findings. In this way, the outputs from consultation with staff help to identify and refine effective people management practices, which are shared throughout the company.

The PFI scores have improved significantly throughout the organisation since its introduction – from 68% favourable to 75% favourable – with particular improvements seen in the range of scores, especially in the bottom quartile group of teams.

Does the PFI matter?

Annual tracking of the progress in PFI findings shows a clear link between action on gaps indicated and improvement in both PFI scores and findings on all other aspects of the staff survey.

Statistical analysis has shown a strong and direct link between effective people management, as evidenced by the PFI levels, to:

- Employee commitment
- Customer satisfaction levels
- Financial performance.

The PFI has thus become an important measurement tool and catalyst for change throughout the organisation.

The PFI is factor-analysed annually and also tested statistically against other aspects of staff's attitudes, to ensure it continues to measure the key drivers of effective People Management. Additionally following its third year, a full external review of the PFI was commissioned, which has further refined both the questions included and the application of the findings.

Future plans

As the survey has become more targeted and issue-specific, the business response and action planning has become more incisive and challenging. It has become clear that many of the issues identified by the survey now are more long-term, and require some time to embed solutions and show impact.

Consequently, a decision was made in mid-2005 to move the main survey to a 2-year cycle, with 25% of the teams also undertaking an interim survey in each intervening year. These teams will be, in the main, those that have shown relatively weak PFI scores in the previous year. The annual survey will continue to provide the PFI findings to these teams, recognising the continued importance of the survey findings in annual tracking and guiding action for those teams that are not performing well on locally-driven aspects.

The interim survey will examine not only the PFI but also other locally-driven aspects. It is not intended that it will generate division or Group reports but only individual team reports. Should there be a need to examine organisation-wide aspects in the intervening years, a facility has been developed to run short sample surveys using the company Intranet.

How does the survey work?

In summary:

- The survey takes place biennially in late Autumn, with team reports available from December.

- Each report shows the findings both by item and by category, and benchmarks each team against its own trend data, against its parent team (for example, region or division) and against stretching external benchmarks.

- Organisation-wide issues are addressed through divisional and cross-functional analysis and action planning, which are often set centrally and cascaded through the organisation.

- The survey findings are shared with all staff, who are then actively involved in prioritisation and action planning based on the findings for their team. A detailed *Guide to Action Planning* has been developed to assist in this task.

- Action planning is SMART and feeds into specific performance objectives for individual members of management and staff.

- The following year, for those teams not being surveyed, progress on action plans is reviewed with HR and senior management, and objectives adjusted accordingly. For those teams participating in the interim survey (and for all teams in a full survey year), the findings are reviewed against objectives, and in this way integrated into the performance management process.

- Teams that require close monitoring and support may be provided with additional analysis through focus groups.

- Specific improvement targets for PFI are established at division and individual team levels from year to year, and monitored closely.

Who is Responsible for What in the Survey Cycle?

While the survey is managed centrally, as it plays a key role in monitoring and driving the People Management programme, both HR teams and business management have significant roles in its application:

- The survey is managed by the small Group Employee Research (GER) team, which is responsible for consultation and development, planning and management, including process design, analysis, business support, and communication of findings at Group and Divisional levels. GER also manages the relationship with the external survey provider, ISR, which works closely with GER in processing of data, production of reports, provision of external norms, and secondary analysis. The team also monitors progress of divisional action plans, reports to top management and the Board bi-annually, and undertakes detailed secondary analysis, interim or targeted surveys, where required.

- Individual co-ordinators in each division carry out local administration, support, and communication roles. In most cases, these co-ordinators are on the HR team.

- HR, both centrally through the divisional HR Business Partners, and locally through HR managers and co-ordinators, provides support to the business on an ongoing basis. This support includes:
    - ◆ Reviewing findings
    - ◆ Quality-checking action plans

- ♦ Coaching and supporting management or teams, where appropriate
- ♦ Monitoring of progress
- ♦ Identification and sharing of best practice.

- HR is also directly responsible for an intensive programme of remedial action required by any teams where findings indicate this is required.

- Line management is the owner of the findings, and is directly responsible to communicate findings, involve staff in analysis and action planning, drive actions, and monitor and report to senior management.

- Senior management reviews team findings with line and HR management, provides management coaching where necessary, sets targets, and carries out quarterly reviews of progress, reporting to top management.

- Staff are directly involved in the prioritisation, action planning, and ongoing monitoring to address issues in their individual teams. Staff are also involved in further issues analysis or in solution design for division-wide or group-wide issues.

Barriers Uncovered & Surmounted

These include:

- **Company culture:** Historically, performance was differentiated and rewarded solely on business results. The introduction of a 'Balanced Scorecard' approach, facilitated by the development of the PFI, was thus counter-cultural. PFI had to be seen to be absolute robust, and to establish clear links between its findings and financial results. Extensive testing (including linkage research), publication of test findings, and regular consultation with the business has overcome this barrier.

- **Inappropriate use of scores:** HR has established strict standards for the use of the PFI requiring consideration of trend analysis, relative positioning *vs* peers, and achievement against targets. HR monitors the use of the PFI closely.

- **Small teams:** Where a manager does not have a team of at least 15, a survey report, and consequently PFI score, will not be produced and so these managers do not have a PFI to be fed into their performance management and reward process. Local intelligence and judgement is used to good effect here.

Continuing progress

The survey overall is not used just as the key people measure in individual and organisational performance measurement. It also provides the information against which the business can assess progress on both short-term and long-term People objectives, and it guides management in introducing business changes, reviewing processes, and assessing impact of initiatives, work-practices, environmental influences, and key strategic programmes. There is a wealth of evidence that such staff consultation adds real value to the business and helps to generate and sustain such factors as employee engagement, and to understand, and therefore to influence, organisational culture.

> 'Once we understand what matters to our staff, we can better address their concerns, to ensure they become more engaged with the organisation and with their work. In this way, not only will they gain more satisfaction and sense of value from working here, but we will benefit from higher commitment, more positive contributions to the organisation, higher trust levels, and higher productivity'.
> **Mike Lewis – Head of Strategic HR, AIB Group**
> **(October 2004)**

Conclusion

The survey in AIB changes each year, with current priorities addressed alongside the classic aspects of working life, which are constantly tracked. Whatever topics covered, the survey findings now form an integral part of the way we work together in AIB.

They are carefully considered, they are analysed in a business-like manner and, most importantly, they are acted upon. This is the real success factor, and perhaps the key differentiator, of the survey in AIB: that it informs decision-making as a positive and pro-active source of business intelligence.

AIB STAFF SURVEY – KEY FEATURES

- The inclusion of all staff in the organisation, and the full sharing of findings with all staff.

- Alignment with strategic business priorities, enabling monitoring of the impact of major change programmes, and adjustment accordingly.

- Provision of tracking data on a range of topics.

- Concentration on follow-up actions and intensive support to line management in this regard.

- The provision of a management index (the *People Focus Index*), which monitors the effectiveness of local management and their role in motivating and managing staff to deliver the business strategy.

- Detailed issues analysis of group and division-wide topics identified by the survey.

- In 2002, a Senior Management Survey was launched as an occasional strategic supplement to the survey.

- Segmentation analysis allows targeted solutions to be designed for key issues identified.

- Key driver analysis is undertaken to identify the drivers of, for example, staff engagement.

CRITICAL SUCCESSFUL FACTORS

- Active and visible sponsorship by senior management.

- Quarterly reviews and published updates.

- Visible action taken and communicated at organisation and team level.

- Direct ownership by teams of their prioritisation and actions.

- Use of *People Focus Index* scores (based on quartile analysis) to inform the Performance Management system.

- Timing of survey: results provided on time to inform business planning, performance reviews and objective-setting.

- Support and endorsement of the Irish Bank Officials Association.

Appendix: How is the PFI Calculated?

The index comprises 18 questions, mostly about 'my immediate manager', all of which have a 5-point response scale. The findings are presented as 'favourable', unfavourable' or 'neutral'. The two positive responses on the scale are amalgamated to generate the 'favourable' scores, and the scores on all 18 questions are simply amalgamated to generate the higher level scores.

So, if a team has a favourable score of 70%, this means that 70% of the team members are positive about the effectiveness of their management team. However, this overall total can mask the ranges in scores across individual questions, so it is this range analysis that is more important. HR mangers do in-depth analysis of each team's findings to identify trends, and strengths and weaknesses. In this way, a manager or management team can identify that, for instance, they are weak on performance management, but strong on work organisation, and the relevant support, training, or management development can be provided.

CASE 2

The Fundamentals & First Time Right:
Applying HR Initiatives to Implement Corporate Strategy at Hibernian Life & Pensions[2]

Hibernian Life & Pensions is Ireland's largest life and pensions broker company and the third largest life & pensions company overall. The product of the merger of Norwich Union, CGU and Hibernian in October 2000, it is one of two subsidiary divisions of the Hibernian Group and is part of the international Aviva Group, the seventh largest insurer in the world.

This case study outlines how, through progressive HR policies, real business change can be facilitated. It demonstrates the techniques used to achieve this and the dramatic changes that happened in Hibernian. This initiative was part of the HR Strategy devised in 2001, of which one of the key responsibilities for HR was to make Hibernian the company everyone wants to work for, providing great jobs and a fun working environment.

In 2001, evidence emerged of two very significant business problems that, if not addressed, would impact the sustainability of the company. First, the merger of three very different cultures had resulted in a disparate, and often conflicting, organisational climate. Secondly, the company's customer service had faltered substantially and excellent customer service became critical to Hibernian's success.

In addition, Hibernian's employee attrition was over 30% in the year 2000 and the company had ranked last for two successive years in the Irish Brokers Association's customer survey.

---

[2] This case study was prepared with the assistance of Alastair McMenamin at Hibernian Life & Pensions.

To meet this challenge, the company launched a Business Excellence initiative. At the suggestion of the HR Director, the senior management team decided to analyse the company's strengths and weaknesses in a fresh way that would specifically address its culture and customer service problems. The Excellence model developed by the European Foundation for Quality Management (EFQM) was identified as a framework that would meet this need.

An analysis of the organisation was conducted using this model, which consisted of in-depth interviews with directors, managers and staff within the company. It identified a number of areas where Hibernian could improve. A 3-day management away day was held to prioritise and gain buy-in for these improvements. Underpinning all of this analysis was a belief in the Roebuck Customer Employee Chain model, which postulates that increased staff satisfaction leads to increased customer satisfaction, which in turn leads to increased profits.

The approach to resolving these issues was to gain as much involvement at as many levels in the organisation as possible. It was also important that the project be as cross-functional as possible. Each project was sponsored by the company's Managing Director.

Two key projects were initiated that aimed to change the culture of the company to drive customer satisfaction:

- The Fundamentals (Culture)
- First Time Right (Customer Service).

It was quickly realised that, to succeed, staff needed to engage significantly in the process. A month-long communication exercise, named 'The Answer', was organised to generate staff ownership of the projects and to make explicit that the answer to the problems the company was facing could only be solved from within.

Following this communication exercise, staff were invited to join the project teams and both initiatives worked as follows.

The Fundamentals

Hibernian Life & Pensions was effectively the combination of three cultures, and had inherited considerably different ways of doing business and working together. It was realised that, if a common culture could be achieved, it would have a huge impact on employee satisfaction and would reduce dramatically the level of employee turnover in the company.

Focus groups were run, with a broad representation of staff of all levels and functions within the organisation to develop the new culture, which was named the 'Fundamentals', based on six key organisational values:

- Customer Excellence
- Participation & Encouragement
- Working Together
- Innovation & Learning
- Empowerment & Responsibility
- Focus on Achievement.

Teams and individuals were then asked to embed the Fundamentals further by writing team charters. Monthly competitions were run to choose the team or individual who best demonstrated the Fundamentals. An awards panel, consisting of staff members nominated by their peers, selected the award winner each month. Awards were presented each month by the Managing Director and an overall awards ceremony was held each year at the Christmas party to decide the 'Supercheque', which is the individual or team who most contributed to the Fundamentals in the past year.

There were fears initially within parts of the organisation that the Fundamentals programme might be perceived as a fad. The Fundamentals team addressed these fears through an extensive communications plan, fortnightly team meetings, and refreshing the team with new representatives annually. Critical to the success of the project was the linkage of the Fundamentals to the reward system of the company. This was made a day-to-day reality by the inclusion of the Fundamentals in the annual objectives section of all staff members. The Fundamentals recognition programme was relaunched in September 2003.

The Fundamentals have become the way that staff work together throughout the company. The new culture is underpinned by a real effort to listen to staff and to make Hibernian a great place to work.

The Premium Policy

The HR department introduced the 'Premium' policy in 2001 to combat the major turnover problems in the company. Four areas for improvement were identified to create a better working environment and these formed the bedrock of the policy.

First, staff had asserted a need for more training and development. A new training strategy was developed, which focused on increasing the capability of staff to meet customer needs. This involved:

- Customer care training
- Product and technical training
- An increased focus on professional exams
- A huge investment in team leader and management training.

Second, there was a lack of clarity about the benefits of working in Hibernian. Extensive communication about the salary review and bonus system and other employee benefits now takes place. Also, following on from feedback in the 2002 employee survey, radical changes to the Performance Management & Reward system were enacted. These changes met the company's and employees' need to reward the higher performers better.

Third, a focus on work / life balance was introduced into the organisation. Hibernian already has a very successful flexi-time system, which led to lower absenteeism throughout the company. This has been enhanced by the addition of initiatives, such as yoga classes and healthy option menus in subsidised canteens.

Finally, a focus on making Hibernian a fun place to work was introduced. This manifested itself in the evening course programme that was developed for staff. Courses available have included belly-dancing, photography and boxercise.

Staff satisfaction and engagement are measured each year in our employee survey. This measures how well the Fundamentals and the Premium policy are being lived in the organisation. After every survey, a strong commitment is made to resolve any issues raised by staff. For instance, as mentioned previously, staff had raised concerns over the level of training and development offered, which resulted in individuals finding it difficult to meet customer requirements through lack of experience and knowledge. To address this, a new training and development strategy was formulated with set targets for increasing employee competency.

First Time Right

The merger of 2000 had caused serious concern over the ability of Hibernian to deliver quality customer service – surveys showed that Hibernian ranked 7th out of the nine life companies in Ireland. Implementing the 'First Time Right' project was considered key to winning the Irish Brokers Association's Service Excellence award for the 'Most Improved' company, a major organisational goal.

The second big challenge was to improve the experience customers were having with Hibernian. The high employee turnover rate in the year 2000 resulted in a large number of inexperienced staff being attached to the Customer Services department. In turn, this resulted in complaints about the quality of work conducted in the company. A blame culture with regard to these quality problems simply exacerbated the problem.

The de Bono 'six hats' technique was used to address this problem. These brainstorming sessions allowed staff members to voice their concerns and to suggest their own solutions to quality issues. Representatives of each team then led the process, with assistance from a co-ordinating cross-functional team. This approach was applied to units as diverse as Premium Collection, Pensions, Actuarial and even the HR department.

The approach allowed for significant changes in processes, with areas now required to measure their inputs and outputs. For example, Life New Business started giving feedback to sales about incomplete applications. This created a need for training in the sales area, which when completed improved quality greatly. The initiative created significant 'buy-in' for quality across the organisation and addressed many of the issues with regard to the blame culture that existed in some areas of the business.

The First Time Right initiative originally experienced a lot of negativity early on, but the use of the de Bono 'six hats' process helped to demonstrate that the initiative would be driven by the needs of individuals within the teams, rather than managers. This convinced staff that First Time Right was to everyone's benefit. As the methodology was introduced to more and more teams, employees became convinced of its benefits and more and more areas of the organisation wanted to get involved.

To keep the focus on quality, Hibernian has been audited each year since 2002 by EFQM. Each year, areas for improvement are identified, prioritised and actions taken. In 2004, we applied for the 'Mark of Excellence' standard from the Excellence Ireland Quality Association. Not only did EIQA award Hibernian this standard but it also named us as its National Quality Award winners for 2004.

Results

It is often very difficult to measure the success of people initiatives. It is even more difficult to link them with concrete business results. However, we were able to track these initiatives through internal targets, which were set, and through external benchmarks – for example:

Culture

- **Best Companies to Work For:** Hibernian was voted among the top 5 of companies to work for with over 1,000 employees in the *Irish Independent*'s "Best Companies to Work for in Ireland" survey in 2003. We have remained as one of the Top 50 companies to work for in Ireland for the past three years.

- **Staff Turnover Rates:** These fell from 35% in 2000, to 16%, 9%, 10% and 10% in the following years. This represented a move from the highest in the Life & Pensions industry to one of the lowest. Since 2002, Hibernian has consistently out-performed industry benchmarks with regard to employee turnover.

Staff Survey Results

- There has been a big turnaround in staff satisfaction across the organisation – from 2001: 56% Favourable (Different survey, composite core used), to 2002: 67% Favourable and 2003: 71% Favourable, which compare favourably with industry benchmarks. In particular, the areas focused on, such as culture, and training and performance management have greatly improved satisfaction scores (**Figure 1**).

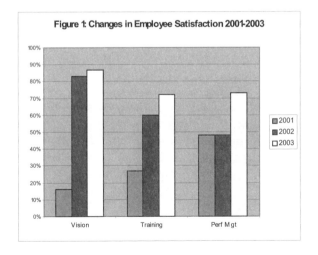

Figure 1: Changes in Employee Satisfaction 2001-2003

Customer Service

- **IBA Results:** Hibernian Life & Pensions won the 'Most Improved Company' in the Irish Brokers Association Service Excellence awards in 2003.

- **Quality Results:** Reduction in errors in new business process fell from 20% to 2%. Overall quality in the customer service area has been maintained over 95% since 2002.

- **EIQA award:** Hibernian won the National Quality Award from the Excellence Ireland Quality Association in October 2004.

CASE 3

The Balanced Scorecard – Supporting HR & Business Excellence at HP Ireland[3]

Hewlett Packard (HP) employs approximately 4,000 people in Ireland across five business units. A Fortune 100 company headquartered in Palo Alto, California, it employs 150,000 people globally. In 2004, the organisation had global revenues of $80 billion. Long-known and recognised for its cultural qualities, referred to as the 'HP Way', it has supplemented this by the application of the 'Balanced Scorecard' within the organisation, which is used by many groups / functions, including HR.

The 'Balanced Scorecard' was first introduced to the business world in a 1992 *Harvard Business Review* article.[4] Since then, it has been applied in countless organisations. Commenting subsequently about their experiences, co-author Norton observed:

> 'the typical executive team has a high degree and awareness and consensus around the financial strategy as well as the priorities for operational process improvement. They typically have limited consensus around customer strategies . . . . But the worst grades are reserved for their understanding of strategies for developing human capital. There is little consensus,

---

[3] This case study was prepared with the assistance of Kevin McNamara, HR Manager at HP Ireland.

[4] Kaplan, Robert S. & Norton, David P. (1992). 'The Balanced Scorecard – Measures that Drive Performance', *Harvard Business Review*, Jan/Feb, pp.71-79.

little creativity and so no real framework for thinking about the subject.'[5]

HP's model demonstrates how it has risen to the challenge posed by Norton. Globally, HP has a leadership framework that acts as an interdependent system. The framework provides a 'line of sight' for the organisation in respect of what they must achieve. The 'Balanced Scorecard' is an integral part of the process.

LEADERSHIP FRAMEWORK

Strategy
> Our corporate objectives
> Our corporate strategy
> Our value proposition

Values & Behaviours
> Our shared values
> Our standards & conduct

Structure & Processes
> Our operating model

Metrics, Results & Rewards
> Our balanced scorecard

Research has demonstrated the power and value of using the 'Balanced Scorecard'. Companies applying a scorecard methodology typically have better business results – for example:

- 83% have financial performance in the top third of their industry
- 74% were perceived as industry leaders by their peers
- 97% were perceived as leaders on changing the nature of their industries.[6]

5   Becker, B.E., Huselid, M.A., & Ulrich, D. (2001). *The HR Scorecard – Linking People, Strategy & Performance*, Boston: Harvard Business School Press.
6   Mercer Delta.

Importantly for organisations where conflicting demands and distractions are plentiful, research has demonstrated that organisations using the balanced scorecard (BSC) report significantly higher strategic alignment and awareness throughout the organisation.

	BSC Company	Non-BSC Company
Agreement between management on strategy	90%	47%
Cooperation and teamwork between management	85%	38%
Open sharing and communication	71%	30%
Effective communication of strategy	60%	8%
High levels of self-monitoring by employees	42%	16%

For HP, the evidence has been compelling and has resulted in its use of the 'Balanced Scorecard' as a strategic management system used to drive performance and accountability. Because of the nature of the model, it can incorporate both the leading and lagging business indicators to predict the current and future performance. At HP, this is reflected as follows:

Financial	Operational Excellence
Customers	Employees

Some of the benefits of this methodology for HP are:

- Alignment of individual and corporate objectives
- Accountability is clear throughout the organisation
- Organisation culture is driven by performance
- Shareholder value is enhanced
- Capacity to track business unit and organisational performance against the strategic objectives
- Reinforce the desired behaviours throughout the organisation.

Research suggests that more of the value created by firms can be attributed to intangibles. Work undertaken by Lev, Huselid, Becker & Beatty clearly stressed the need to nurture, retain and motivate the intellectual capital of the firm. HR professionals are uniquely placed to contribute to the firm's value creation, if they can harness this aspect and apply appropriate systems.

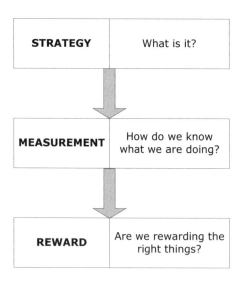

A line of sight is facilitated by the application of the scorecard at HP to achieve a high performance workplace. On a financial year basis, corporate / business objectives are cascaded down to business units / regions, then they continue to be cascaded until they manifest in individual performance plans. The achievement of the performance objectives leads to a total reward outcome that is a combination of pay and non-pay items.

At HP, 'cascading' is not just an expression to convey the dissemination of the plan. It refers explicitly to the development of the 'Balanced Scorecard' deeper into the organisation to encourage and to align individual actions that contribute to the accomplishment of the strategic objectives. Execution is not left to chance, but is the clear responsibility of the 'Balanced Scorecard' leader in each unit.

For HP, the 'Balanced Scorecard' is the critical bridge that translates strategic objectives into individual actions and behaviours linking corporate strategy to the 'Balanced Scorecard', to individual performance plans, ensuring that everyone is working towards not only common goals, but the right goals.

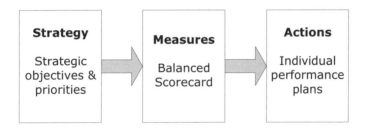

Within the HP organisation, a need was raised by staff through the 'Voice of the Workforce' survey for a means of managing performance. The 'Balanced Scorecard' approach facilitates the roll-out of a real-time performance management tool (PMP) that achieves cost savings through improved productivity, quality, cost-per-call and customer satisfaction.

The objectives of the 'Balanced Scorecard' included:

- Balanced performance: productivity *and* quality
- Customer focus
- Consistent evaluation and standards of performance
- Shift from supervising to leading people

- Linking individual performance to business goals
- Linking achievement with reward
- Development planning.

Many organisations are faced with the same problems as HP in respect of performance management. The system is designed, rolled out in a fanfare and then withers. For performance management to be meaningful and value-creating, it must integrate into the business.

To affirm the 'Balanced Scorecard', HP represents the benefits of the PMP in that model. Therefore, there can be no ambiguity about measurements, metrics or value creation. HP advocates the benefits of balance and the 'Balanced Scorecard' illustrates the point.

Financial > Directly link individual performance to reward > Reduces operating costs > Strategic analysis	**Operational Excellence** > Productivity driver > 360° feedback tools > Comparator
Customer > Competitive advantage > Winning customer deals > Commitment to HP's customer's goals	**Employees** > Performance review > Poor performers > Talent management

Despite having developed such an information-rich tool, HP's journey has not ended. Recently, a senior HP VP challenged the HR group to 'produce the HR metrics'. For many organisations, the present state would equate to the end state. Not at HP, where the journey takes a new direction.

Much research has been undertaken on the metrics of HR and Beatty, Huselid and Schneier have developed an interesting framework.[7] They propose that the employee quadrant or "workforce success" is comprised of shared mindset, competences and behaviours that are determined by the firm's strategy / value proposition. Their workforce success is supported by HR competencies, system and practice. These items then form the HR scorecard embedded in the 'Balanced Scorecard'. This represents the way forward for HP and others who want to determine the value and contribution of their most significant asset.

---

[7]   Beatty, R.W., Huselid, M.A., Schneier, C.E. (2003). 'The New HR Metrics: Scoring on the Business Scorecard', *Organisational Dynamics*, Vol.32, No.32, pp.107-121.

3

RECRUITMENT &
RETENTION

The lifeblood of knowledge economies is not technology; it is knowledge workers. Attracting and recruiting the best employees is critical to success in all sectors and to all types of organisation, regardless of size. The current employment climate is once again undergoing a period of rapid growth. We began the IMI *Management Recruitment Index* in October 2003, with a view to capturing a figure that could be used as an indicator for the availability of management positions available in Ireland. Eighteen months later, the activity captured in this index had more than doubled. IMI's most recent survey of MNCs in Ireland (2005), which has been conducted over the last 8 years, recorded a growing concern with the availability of labour in Ireland. Economic data from a number of sources are reporting greater availability of jobs, which creates difficulties for recruiters who are forced to compete for smaller supplies of labour, and for organisations that seek to retain employees who are more empowered to switch organisations.

Michaels *et al.* (2001) captured this situation excellently in their phrase 'the war for talent'. Written during the heady dot.com days, it pays credence to the reality that many companies continue to face: key employees are an organisation's central resource, and losing them hurts the organisation more than any other business setback. In her seminal text on innovation and knowledge management, Leonard-Barton (1995) writes:

'... firms are knowledge, as well as financial, institutions. They are repositories and wellsprings of knowledge. Expertise collects in employees' heads and is embodied in machines, software, and routine organisational processes. Some of this knowledge and know-how is essential simply to survive or to achieve parity with the competition. However, it is *core* or *strategic* capabilities that distinguish a firm competitively. Management of these strategic knowledge assets determines the company's ability to survive, to adapt, to compete.'

Whether employees are conceptualised as strategic knowledge assets or as talent, the crucial point is this: recruitment is the most important resource selection activity that any organisation invests time and energy in. Individual knowledge and creativity cannot be replicated elsewhere – if an organisation has this in the form of employees, it belongs exclusively to the organisation and cannot be replicated elsewhere. This is why, even during times of downsizing in organisations, that talent needs to be brought on board.

Assuming that, once talent is attracted and captured, it will stay is a massive mistake. Creating an environment where employees *want* to stay is an essential element of strategic recruitment. Both, in fact, are different sides of the same coin. Strategic recruitment without a retention strategy is a waste of time and resources.

Look at the language used by any employee who is considering ending their contract with an organisation: 'I love my job, but I can't work in this place any longer'. They are stating that they identify with the work they do and get personal satisfaction out of helping the company to meet its aims. The organisation, however, has treated them in a way that means they take their talents elsewhere and pass on the benefits of having a highly-motivated, committed and value-creating employee to a competitor. Consider the impact that losing a valued employee has on the employees who remain.

How many organisations make a substantial investment in attracting and recruiting talent, and subsequently treat that talent as if they are privileged to work there? Employee retention, in short, needs to be as proactive as recruitment. Strategic retention is clearly an issue related to the topics covered in the previous section and throughout this book.

Greville and Barry (2001) carried out an extensive study on the role of strategic retention in Irish organisations, and distilled sixteen retention 'hits' that successful organisations used to keep their best people, which fell within broadly under the general headings of career development, rewards, management and work environment / culture. These 'hits' or recommendations are:

- Autonomy for employees to self-manage their training and development plans.
- Commitment to develop employees' marketability.
- Regular performance reviews.
- Accelerated career progression programmes for star employees.
- Flexible benefits that suit the employee's lifestyle.
- Bonus schemes linked to performance reviews.
- Targeted retention rewards.
- Share options.
- Clear statement of vision and excellent internal communications.
- Respect for people.
- Excellent HR and line manager support for all employees.
- Management with excellent interpersonal skills.
- Culture of honesty that gives employees 'reasons to stay rather than reasons not to go'.
- Work / life balance initiatives.
- Culture of coaching and mentoring.
- Challenging work environment, with a good atmosphere of teamwork and support.

Retention is thus a complex, and far-reaching, issue and requires considerable amounts of energy and initiative on the behalf of organisations. If ignored, it will lead individuals, who are increasingly likely to take responsibility for their own career development, to leave the organisation. If fostered, positive retention strategies will not only assist organisations to hold on to their talent, but will serve ultimately to attract more into the organisation.

With a growing number of jobs becoming available, it is important to recognise that this creates recruitment supply-chain difficulties for organisations. Rapid turnaround times in advertising positions, processing applications, interviewing and selecting the right candidates are vital to ensure that talent is brought into the organisation before they are attracted elsewhere. Internet and e-recruitment technologies have assisted the reduction of recruitment cycle-time enormously and the case on Oracle Ireland's implementation of an interactive web-based recruitment system exemplifies good practice in using technology to meet a strategic human resource need.

The other side of the coin of recruitment is retention: the creation of environments and cultures where employees want to stay is crucial to making sure that the 'wins' achieved by best recruitment practice are not lost. The second case in this chapter focuses on the Hilton Hotel Group's Employee Club initiative in an industry that faces significant challenges in the area of key employee retention (McLaughlin & Cullen, 2003).

References

Greville, M. & Barry, F. (2001). *Capturing the Talent: Is it Finders Keepers? Strategic Retention*, Dublin: IMI.

Leonard-Barton, D. (1995). *Wellsprings of Knowledge: Building and Sustaining the Sources of Innovation*, Boston: Harvard University Press.

McLaughlin, A. & Cullen, J. (2003). *Managers and Work / Life Balance: The Case of the Irish Hospitality Industry*, Dublin: IMI / Irish Hotel & Catering Institute.

Michaels, E., Handfield-Jones, H. & Axelrod, B. (2001). *The War for Talent*, Boston: Harvard Business School Press.

O'Connor, M. (2005). *Survey of MNCs in Ireland: Results of the 8th Annual Survey of Competitiveness*, Dublin: IMI / Irish Independent.

CASE 4

The Implementation of an Interactive

Web-based Recruitment System at Oracle Ireland[8]

Oracle's business is information – how to manage it, use it, share it, protect it. For nearly three decades, Oracle, the world's largest enterprise software company, has provided the software and services that let organisations get the most up-to-date and accurate information from their business systems. Headquartered in Redwood Shores, California, Oracle employs more than 50,000 professionals in 100+ countries around the world. Oracle's presence in Ireland is split into six main operations, employing 950 people.

In December 1999, Oracle Ireland decided to move from a stand-alone database system to an interactive web-based recruitment system to meet the specialist needs of a fast-paced function and to propel Oracle Ireland Recruitment into the position of best practice market-leaders in eRecruitment within the Irish market place.

In order to achieve the timely, cost-effective, quality hiring of over 500 multi-lingual, multi-skilled employees and process approximately 12,000 applications *per annum*, it became essential to harness the potential of web-based recruitment methods.

The business case for implementing the system was based on four key areas:

1. Cost Reduction

- The system allowed more efficient candidate processing, in particular where jobs have a high volume of applications. This

---

[8]   This case study was prepared with the assistance of Sonya Mahood, Recruitment Manager for Ireland, Oracle Ireland.

improved operational efficiency and resulted in a saving on labour time in transaction-based, lower level processing and allowed resources to work on projects that add more value to the business.

- The web was beginning to become the main avenue used by candidates seeking a new job. With this change in the market-place, by harnessing web-based technology, the business decreased reliance on other, more costly sourcing methods, such as recruitment agencies and newspaper advertising.

2. Reports & Analysis

- Automated reports on Key Performance Metrics allowed the analysis of key data to measure the efficiency of the department and allow for ongoing enhancement and changes to processes. Reports could be run to analyse the following:
  - ◆ *Candidate Source Information:* Time to Hire; Vacancy Reports; Headcount Planning.
  - ◆ *Candidate Management:* Tracked and managed candidates for headcount planning and forecasting; Increased customer service to candidates.

3. Standardise

- Automated and standardised the business processes across EMEA (Europe Middle East & Africa).
- Generated system Service Levels for all stages of the process.
- Increased customer service to hiring managers and vendors with a standard process.
- Provided instant access to accurate, consolidated information to meet legal and regulatory mandates for corporate performance management and responsibility.

4. Win the war for talent

- Accessed the global network and extended Oracle's Recruitment reach.

- Increased volume of relevant applicants.
- Enhanced company profile.

Alignment with Overall Business Objectives

The initiative was in line with the overall strategic business objectives.

At a global level, the vision of Oracle's CEO, Larry Ellison, was to be Number One in eBusiness and for Oracle to be an eBusiness. Oracle was standardising processes across operations on a global basis and the implementation of a web-based system in Ireland and across EMEA would allow for business process, hiring and candidate application systems to be standardised across all participating countries.

Oracle also wanted to develop its 'recruitment brand' and sought to attract the best people in the market-place in line with the HR goal of attracting, retaining and motivating the best people.

Oracle is a learning organisation, and global access by employees with clear visibility on opportunities internally for career progression was perceived as a priority.

Overall HR objectives

These included:

- **Staff Retention & Employee Development:** Promoting opportunities globally enabled Oracle to retain the best talent within the organisation and to encourage employee development. Employees were also rewarded through the online referral scheme – a financial incentive for employees who recommend a candidate to Oracle who is then hired.

- **Professionalism & Confidentiality:** Transferring Business Processes to a system and tracking of Service Levels ensured a professional level of customer service for applicants and vendors. The online tracking of interviews and restricted access to the system ensured customer confidentiality.

- **Work-Life Balance:** Flexible working was facilitated, as employees can log onto a web-based recruitment system from any computer with Internet access.
- **Equal Opportunities:** The recruitment process was equitable and visible to all external and internal candidates.

Key personnel involved in the initiative included the Oracle recruitment team (who were responsible for driving and project-managing the initiative), hiring managers, IT Department, HR management, heads of the lines of business.

The project was implemented over the following timescale:

Date	Milestones
December 1999	Decision to move to web-based recruitment. Conception of strategic plan.
December 1999 – August 2000	Transition from email and paper-based recruitment process to web-based fully-integrated system.
July 2000	Mapping, integration, adoption and enhancement of existing processes to web-based system.
August 2000	Web-based system implemented. All applications (candidates / agencies / internal applicants and employee referrals) now driven through the web.

The following ensured the sustainability of the initiative within the organisation over the longer term:

- **Training:** Oracle employees at all levels are trained and educated on the web-based process of application for both internal career opportunities and the referral of potential candidates to Oracle. All agency partners also receive training on the process of submitting candidates online.
- **Online Application:** All applicants are directed to the online application process and advised that this is the recognised application process for Oracle, highlighting the benefits to the employee of managing their application online at http://jobs.oracle.ie.

- **Global web culture:** The alignment of the initiative with Oracle's organisational goal 'to be an eBusiness' ensures a lack of resistance to the system within the organisation.

Evaluation of the Project

The following tools / processes were used to evaluate the success of the project:

- **Service Levels:** Internal Service Levels were determined for all applications to Oracle Ireland. The system automatically generates alerts as Service Levels become due. This ensures all applicants receive prompt and timely feedback and have a satisfactory encounter with the Oracle recruitment team. For example, once a candidate interviews with Oracle, an alert is generated to prompt the Recruitment Consultant to give the candidate feedback within three days.

- **Time to Hire:** This monitors the length of time a position is open, from the day the vacancy is approved, to candidate identification and offer contract signed.

- **Cost per hire metrics:** Measures the total cost to Oracle of each employee recruited, factoring in all contributing costs – for example, resource allocation, advertising, etc.

- **Applications online *vs* other methods:** Monitors number of online applications *versus* applications received through other avenues, such as email and hard copy.

- **Source Reports:** Monitors the volume of hires from various sources and allows Recruitment to monitor agency hires compared to direct sources for each line of business.

- **Application Numbers:** Measures the number of applicants for each open position.

Benefits to the Organisation

The recruitment process is now a paperless process, with a reduced transaction time. The implementation of the system resulted in decreased cost per hire, due to a combination of factors

– in particular, reduced spend on traditional advertising methods, decrease in the percentage of agency hires and an increase in the number of quality applicants.

The success of implementing a web-based Recruitment system has improved Oracle's image as an employer in the market place and its reputation as a true eBusiness. It ensures that the candidate's experience of the recruitment process is smooth and seamless, as well as timely for the organisation. Response times are much faster for both planned and unexpected headcount requirements, thus significantly reducing our time to hire. It has empowered employees to take ownership of individual career development.

Return on Investment

The initiative has succeeded in achieving each of the predetermined performance objectives:

- **Cost Reduction:** The number of hires where candidates were sourced from an agency decreased by 50% over a three-year period. In conjunction with the system rollout, Oracle implemented a preferred supplier listing (PSL) with selected agencies, enabling discounted rates across all positions. All agencies on the PSL submitted applications online to specific jobs. Also the Oracle online application is linked to several job boards globally, driving candidate traffic and active job-seekers to the Oracle site. This resulted in the following:

  ♦ The volume of applications to Oracle Ireland increased by 150%.

  ♦ Labour time and cost reduced, as a Recruitment Administrator previously had to upload all submissions from job boards and agencies to a stand-alone database. Prior to Q4 2001, a full-time resource was required to upload applicant CVs.

  ♦ Increased efficiency of candidate management and pipeline generation of candidates for future vacancies. All applications are directed to apply by either the internal or external websites. Oracle has alternative application methods for individuals who do not have access to the web; this portion is less than 1% of overall application numbers.

- **Reports & Analysis:** Monthly and weekly reports are run on key performance indicators, which in turn enables Oracle to continuously 'sharpen the sword' in relation to recruitment processes. A number of enhancements and changes have been made since the implementation of the system, which would not have been previously measurable.

- **Standardise:** The application and recruitment process is now standardised within EMEA, allowing for a consistent and user-friendly application process for both internal and external candidates. Service Level Agreements are in place for each stage of the Recruitment Process. Accurate tracking information on each candidate and role is recorded. A standard process has encouraged collaboration between countries, and the web-based application has enabled recruitment consultants to work across different countries with colleagues based remotely.

- **To win the war for talent:** At the time of implementation, there were limiting market factors that caused a serious shortage of available qualified candidates in Ireland. Implementing the online system increased Oracle's access to a global skills pool, thereby enabling it to hire the best possible candidates at the lowest possible cost in the quickest possible time. The profile of Oracle as an employer in the Irish market-place was significantly raised.

Impact on Employees

Impacts included:

- **Empowering the Employee**: The system enables all employees to create and update their own profiles and be alerted automatically to new opportunities. This has transformed the quantity and process of internal transfers. In 2003, internal moves accounted for 30% of all hires.

- **Consistency of Hiring Process:** Adherence to procedures generated by the system ensures all internal applicants experience a similar process. This has eliminated inconsistent hiring scenarios and ensures all employees have visibility of opportunities.

- **Referral Process:** Employees can refer friends through the system by providing a name and email address. This is a simple process for the employee and ensures that they receive payment if the referral is successful. The visibility of the process means it is widely used.

Summary

As with many global organisations, in the year 2000 Oracle Corporation faced increasing recruitment costs and lead times in the quest to source suitably qualified candidates. Implementation of the web-based system has allowed the company to respond quickly and effectively to growing demands in an increasingly competitive international labour market, ensuring both increased efficiency and a major cost saving to the organisation.

CASE 5

The Hilton Group's Employee Club[9]

The hotel sector has always faced huge challenges in terms of the availability of personnel. The business is largely a 24-hour, 365-day per year industry, and many jobs offer more sociable hours, often with less customer-facing demands. Despite the large number of challenges faced in the context of staff retention in the hospitality sector, it is a working environment that is attractive to high-energy managers who have an interest in working with a range of clients. A difficulty exists, however, in retaining people in an environment that is faced with considerable competition.

Despite huge staff retention challenges in the hospitality sector over the past number of years, and the enduring image of hotels as 'difficult' environments in which to work, the Hilton Hotel Group has ranked in the top Irish 50 places to work over the last two years.

Internationally, Hilton has around 680 properties outside Ireland and is one of the most recognisable and well-regarded hotel chains in the world. It will soon launch its second property in Ireland.

The Hilton Employee Club has a number of purposes. It was set up to foster a spirit of camaraderie amongst staff (it was originally known as 'Esprit' or 'Spirit of the Hilton'), but also gives clear and valuable benefits to members, who receive a Hilton Club Card, which entitles the holder to discounts on hotel accommodation around the world in any Hilton hotel. Friends or relatives of card-holders are also entitled to discount on rooms, as well as a 50% discount on hotel food and drink. The offer is open

---

9 This case study was prepared with the assistance of David Webster, General Manager, Hilton Dublin Airport.

to staff, depending on availability (during times when occupancy is below 90%) to ensure there is no revenue lost to the organisation. Every Hilton hotel must participate in the scheme and managers are scored on how many of their staff are members.

Membership of the scheme is dependent on employees meeting retention criteria. Membership is not available to employees upon joining; a three-month induction period has to be completed first. Training on health and hygiene, good work practice, the Hilton culture, etc., has to be completed and signed off by their manager. Upon joining the Hilton Employee Club, shopping vouchers are given to staff as a welcome to the Club and the organisation. Different levels of membership of the Hilton Club are available, which depend on how long an employee has been with the company. The longer the membership, the more benefits employees are entitled to, which facilitates greater retention rates.

The Hilton Employee Club plays an important role in the Group's 'Balanced Scorecard' approach to managing the organisation. Employee satisfaction rates are surveyed twice each year.

Since the goals of the Hilton Group are not focused on short-term profit, the 'Balanced Scorecard' aligns with the philosophy of how the Group wants to work. A key Hilton objective is to be known as the industry leader in customer service excellence. The Group is a people-led business and the retention of quality staff is mission-critical to its continued success. Therefore, the positives of working for the group are continually stressed by, and to, employees. The Group offers opportunities to work in a variety of different countries, as well as to engage in significant self-development.

The Hilton Employee Club is more than a means of incentivising staff to stay with the organisation in terms of reward. It also gives something back to employees, which they can share with families and friends. Membership of the club is dependent on learning about the organisation and its culture, which deepens the relationship between the employee and the organisation. It allows employees to become clients, in a way that tacitly transmits knowledge of customer expectations of the Hilton Group. In a sector where retention is an ongoing concern, the Hilton Employee Club initiative is an innovative example of how an organisation can create bonds with employees that competitors find difficult to match.

4

LEARNING IN
ORGANISATIONS

Intentional or not, learning is something that happens all the time in organisations. Edgar Schein's statement that 'an organisation's culture can be understood as the sum total of learning acquired in an organisational unit' is testimony to this. In knowledge economies, learning is increasingly central to the organisational survival. Charles Leadbeater (2003) has written of a future where creativity and capacity to learn will be central to how we work successfully: 'Entrepreneurship and learning need to become mass, everyday activities' (p.216).

'The Learning Organisation' and 'Organisational Learning' have proven to be enduring concepts since the 1970s. The linking of learning to the development of competitive advantage now has become something of a given. It is evident that the benefits the organisation gets from having employees who are continually engaged in learning activities, be they formal or informal, play a role in organisation renewal and the production of knowledge as a strategic resource.

Moreover, learning initiatives are essential to ensure that organisations can innovate and survive. Harvard Business School Professor Christopher Argyris has been at the forefront of explaining how organisational structure and culture can impede real learning in organisations that facilitate leaving established, self-perpetuating patterns of behaviour (single-loop learning) behind, but also creatively make and enact new initiatives (double-loop learning).

It is interesting that the experts on organisational learning link learning with innovation, creativity and the future of the organisation. *Fifth Discipline* author, Peter Senge, describes a learning organisation as one which is 'continually expanding to create its future'. An organisation's investment in its employees' learning should not be considered a soft HR initative; it is crucial to developing and retaining talent, and to assisting the spread of innovation. In his report on Irish productivity for Microsoft (2005), economist Paul Tansey states:

> 'Additional public investment is required in the human capital domain in order to enhance the knowledge and skills of tomorrow's workforce. In the education sphere, this requires a renewed emphasis on quality of provision. In the training sphere, a major effort is needed to raise the capability of those who are already in employment but possess low skills and few educational qualifications.'

Encouraging learning, education and training is not needed just by organisations; it is an economic imperative for Ireland as it faces the challenge of moving up the value-chain towards its desired destiny as a key player in the global knowledge economy.

A relatively recent development in educational theory has been the concept of lifelong learning. The model of education being provided in youth and early adulthood, prior to formally entering the workplace, and only occasionally being topped-up, is truly defunct. The range of opportunities to learn has become much wider and accessible than before. This matches the hunger for continual learning, which is asserting itself across society. This democratization of the 'social learning space' can only serve to raise the bar on everyone's learning expectations. Organisations will not compete solely on the basis of their knowledge capital, but also on their learning capacity – how its members are encouraged and facilitated in their learning, and how this learning is received, rewarded and integrated into the organisation's future. The lifelong learning movement has done much to normalise 'learning spaces' for groups who were once known as non-traditional learners. Not so long ago, classrooms and training centres had an almost monocultural demographic: certain age groups populated most of the seats. Now, walk into any training or educational institute and far more diversity is evident.

It is widely acknowledged that 70% of learning happens informally, on-the-job (Horibe, 1999). Increasingly, training and education, as opposed to learning, is happening at dispersed and non-traditional centres. This is to facilitate the training needs of workers who, for whatever reason, find access to training centres more difficult. Web-based, e-learning technologies, and distance-education courses have done much to address this divide, but one of the cases discussed here outlines how a learning initiative was delivered to learners in working environments where, traditionally, new knowledge transfer had been almost impossible, due to the operating environment of the particular sector.

The two cases presented here discuss learning in organisational contexts in two very different guises. The first case, the Flour Confectioners & Bakers Association / Skillnets Project, reports how difficulties with providing formal opportunities to learning in busy and dispersed working environments was overcome with an innovative approach. The second case looks at how a programme of lifelong learning has been embedded in a large subsidiary of a multinational pharmaceutical firm, Abbott Ireland. Although the programmes and organisations involved are quite different, both emphasise the importance of providing learning opportunities to staff to meet changes in the competitive landscape and to enrich the lives of employees.

References

Argyris, C. & Schon, D. (1978). *Organisational Learning: A Theory of Action Perspective*. Reading, MA: Addison Wesley Longman Publishing.

Horibe, F. (1999). *Managing Knowledge Workers: New Skills & Attitudes to Unlock the Intellectual Capital in Your Organisation*, New York: John Wiley & Sons.

Leadbeater, C. (2003). *Up the Down Escalator: Why the Global Pessimists Are Wrong*, London: Penguin.

Schein, E. (1996). 'Three Cultures of Management: The Key to Organisational Learning', *Sloan Management Review*, Fall, pp.9-20.

Senge, P. (1990). *The Fifth Discipline: The Art & Practice of the Learning Organisation*, New York: Doubleday.

Tansey, P. (2005). *Productivity: Ireland's Economic Imperative: A Study of Ireland's Productivity Performance and the Implications for Ireland's Future Economic Success*, Dublin: Microsoft Ireland.

CASE 6

The Flour Confectioners & Bakers Association / Skillnets Project: Delivering Training to Dispersed Learning Centres[10]

The wide geographical spread of bakery businesses resulted in a situation where many industry employees had received no formal training or qualifications. Research conducted by the Flour Confectioners & Bakers Association (FCBA) determined that over 80% of people working in the industry had not participated in any form of structured training, despite an overwhelming necessity for the acquisition of baking crafts skills and knowledge. More recently, increased competition from supermarkets, imports and other suppliers of bakery-related food products has already resulted in many closures.

In response to industry needs and requirements for in-house work-based training of the craft skills and knowledge in the manufacture of bread and confectionery, the FCBA, in partnership with Skillnets, set about providing this much sought-after type of training. The key issue faced was that, although a bakery school exists in Dublin, access to this resource was limited on the grounds of the geographical spread of the industry and difficulties with entry levels. The FCBA consulted with its members and determined that the solution was the development of primarily in-house work-based training initiatives. The organisation received funding from Skillnets and appointed a project manager who formed a network of bakeries, recruited a

---

[10]   This case study was prepared with the assistance of Patrick Garvey, Secretary / P.R.O. at the Flour Confectioners & Bakers Association.

panel of highly-skilled industry trainers and put them through an intensive three-week 'train the trainer' course. Training materials were assembled, and two training programmes (*Bread Baking & Processing* and *Bread & Confectionery Manufacturing*) were developed.

From the outset, the initiative aimed to have a strong emphasis on health, safety and hygiene. Moreover, it sought to provide training for employees that was business-friendly and work-based, in order to align with daily production targets.

The network was divided into five smaller network groups and a trainer was appointed to each of these. Training was delivered for four hours per week at each bakery premises, with 1.5 hours dedicated to theory and 2.5 hours focusing on practical 'hands on' skills development. A reporting system, with a weekly report from the trainers and bakery managers, was implemented. During the delivery of the programme, the two modules were accepted for Further Education & Training Awards Council (FETAC) certification.

The examination process also focused on the practical implementation of the skills-based programme. Alongside a classroom-based theoretical exam, practical skills development was assessed by video-taping demonstrations by learners, which accounted for 70% of marks allocated.

Skillnets offered support for the programme, which enabled it to be run out over a 24-month timeframe. The initiative, however, assumed a life of its own and continues to offer training in a number of bakeries across Ireland. Industry stakeholders agreed to continue to fund the initiative when resources ran out.

Participating bakeries have noted that having properly-trained staff not only guarantees better products, manufactured more efficiently, and with a greater awareness of cost effectiveness, but it also allows greater levels of innovation and new product development, which is essential to compete with high-levels of imported bakery and confectionery product coming into the Irish market. Greater varieties of products are now developed indigenously, particularly in the area of speciality breads and confectionery designed to meet the demands of the diversified tastes of a more sophisticated population and also ethnic groupings who are new to Ireland.

On an employee level, a number of the certified trainees have achieved promotion within their organisations and several others now mentor new recruits to the industry. Trained staff have now greater mobility and many are now in a position to move from large plant bakeries to smaller craft bakeries, or to even start their own bakery. The newly-trained bakers find themselves in a stronger financial position, with many of them being remunerated for their achievements and experiencing improved status in their workplaces.

Participating bakeries in the programme have said that there has been a huge return on their investment in the initiative, which has proven to be an innovative way of bringing quality, relevant training to a 'hard-to-reach' learning market.

CASE 7

Lifelong Learning in Abbott Ireland[11]

Abbott Ireland has had a strong tradition of employee development during its 30 years in the Northwest of Ireland, and promotes a philosophy of continuous improvement and lifelong learning. The three aspects of the Lifelong Learning Programme (LLP) discussed here are:

- General Operative Employee Development Programme
- Master of Science in Innovation Management
- Certificate in Maintenance Technology.

The aim of the LLP is to have an active succession plan, which enables Abbott employees to develop and manage their careers, and provide Abbott with skilled internal candidates to fill future vacancies. This initiative is applicable to general operatives, semi-skilled employees, and senior and middle management and is led by Human Resources.

The initiative was implemented over the following time scales:

Learning Initiative	Implementation Timescale
General Operative Employee Development Programme	6 months
Master of Science in Innovation Management	2 years
Certificate in Maintenance Technology	2 years

---

[11] This case study was prepared with the assistance of the HR Department in Abbott Ireland.

Objectives of the Initiative

During the period 2001 to 2003, Abbott's Hospital Products Organisation experienced levels of turnover in line with the national average. The three plants were operating in a very competitive market environment, resulting in a headcount freeze, while the search for new business and products continued.

The key objectives of the LLP are to:

- Reduce staff turnover
- Fill vacancies internally
- Advance employees skills through training and development
- Provide employees with the tools to deal more effectively with change in the workplace.

In preparing the General Operative Employee Development programme (GOED), Abbott benchmarked a number of companies similar in size and nature to Abbott. No company was found that had such a defined and structured employee development programme for its general operative staff. Within the banking sector, there was a similar programme for middle management who had aspirations for senior bank manager roles but no similar programmes for general operatives in similar size organisations in the sector were identified.

Alignment of the Initiative with Overall Business Objectives

The GOED and Certificate in Maintenance Technology programmes afforded the organisation the opportunity to reduce turnover among operatives by providing opportunities to realise potential by completing higher skilled work. Having developed a highly skilled pool of employees from the operative ranks, when employees left the company these vacancies could be filled immediately from an internal pool. This provided employees with development opportunities and was more cost-effective: positions were filled rapidly and recruitment costs were significantly reduced.

The purpose of the MSc was to provide senior and middle managers with the skills to attract new business and the ability to lead the entire workforce through a period of change as the product mix undergoes alteration.

Contribution of the Initiative to the Company's Goals

The initiative has contributed in a number of ways to meeting the organisation's objectives. Since it began, 18 managers have graduated with an MSc. in Innovation Management, 7 operatives have graduated with a Certificate in Maintenance Technology and 32 employees completed the GOED programme. Subsequently, a mentoring programme was introduced and expanded to graduate employees. Perhaps the most significant achievement was the rapid reduction in employee turnover. Additionally, the financial plan and customer service level plans were achieved and significant cost-savings were made. Quality performance improved and the organisation successfully passed the Quality Assurance Corporate Audit. All the above was achieved while operating under a recruitment freeze.

The LLP demonstrated to the Abbott Corporation that the Irish workforce was highly-educated, flexible and responsive to change, which was a factor leading to the further investment by Abbott in the Northwest region – $50 million pharmaceutical plant constructed, $80 million expansion of the Cootehill plant and a doubling of diagnostic workforce from 300 to 600.

Actions have also been taken to sustain the learning momentum provided by the initiative:

- Participants on the GOED programme presented six-monthly updates to the senior plant team.
- Participants on the GOED programme created and manned a presentation stand in the plant canteen, which displayed details of the GOED and outlined the success of this initiative.

This helped raise the profile of the GOED and also afforded participants on the programme the opportunity to inform their peers of the programme's benefits.

- Regular meetings were held with the course leaders for the MSc and Certificate in Maintenance Technology programmes, to improve the course through feedback.

- A graduation ceremony attended by DCU staff was held on-site for the Certificate in Maintenance Technology and an article appeared in the local newspaper describing the event and Abbott's commitment to Lifelong Learning. This significantly raised the profile of the course.

- Articles by participants on Abbott's Lifelong Learning Programme describing the experiences were published in the company magazine, which is distributed to all employees.

Evidence of how the initiative aligned with the overall goals of HR in Abbott Ireland is evident through the high number of internal promotions of the LLP participants. The overall skill level and extent of teamworking within the plant has increased significantly as a result of the programme, and a succession planning process has been fully used.

The mission of HR in Abbott Ireland is 'to create a human organisation capable of being the world's premier health care company'. In 2002, Abbott Ballytivnan was awarded the prestigious title of being Abbott's 'Premier Large Manufacturing Plant' in Abbott's International Division. This award was based on its superior performance in the areas of:

- Lifelong Learning
- Employee Training & Development
- Environmental Health & Safety
- Quality of Product
- Customer Service
- Plant Performance
- Community Involvement.

Participants on the programme have not only attained increased self-confidence as a result of the initiative (a large number of employees have been promoted for the first time in their careers); they have also identified strong career paths and are furthering their careers by continuing their participation in additional education, sponsored by the company.

5

WORK / LIFE BALANCE

'Our research points out very clearly that managers play a critical role in workers' ability to manage their work and personal responsibilities. They're the translators of the corporate culture and the gatekeepers to flexible work options and innovative family friendly policies. By not supporting workers with personal / family commitments, managers lose, employees lose and the company loses.' (Milne, 1999).

In 2003, Marion O'Connor at the IMI Centre for Management Research surveyed a range of managers on the key management, marketplace and personal challenges they faced. It is not surprising that the number one personal challenge faced by the survey population was in achieving a work / life balance. The enormous social change experienced over the last few decades has had a profound impact on traditional careers and on every organisation. One of the most established global experts on organisational health and wellbeing, Professor Cary Cooper, has written:

'The last half of the 20th century has seen enormous change in the nature of society, and of the workplace in particular. In the 1960s, Prime Minister Harold Wilson in the UK talked about the "white heat of technology" transforming our lives, producing the 24-hour week. New technology was going to be responsible for a "leisure age", allowing us to pursue our dreams, even midweek. But instead, the 1970s brought industrial unrest and conflict, a workplace not knowing what it was going to produce or how it was going to do it.' (Cooper, 1998)

Couple this with the rate of transformation in Irish society over the last 10 years (described by sociologist Michel Peillon as 'deep, intense and rapid' (2002)). The time and commitment that organisations require of their members has grown, leaving employees with less time for non-work, non-organisation activities. The rapid acceleration of the rate at which house prices increase is forcing more and more families to locate outside Dublin and other Irish cities, with the result that average commuting times to places of work has grown. The road transport infrastructure is overburdened, so that those who do live in our cities face even more time away from their homes, often stuck in traffic. As a nation, we seem to be suffering from chronic work / life imbalance. We may be highly-motivated and enjoy our jobs but, as human beings, we still want to enjoy our non-work lives. This national work / life imbalance offers a clear opportunity to those workplaces that can meet the family and life needs of their employees, to attract and recruit the employees they want.

Work / life balance is one of the most significant concerns to organisations and the individuals working in them. With predicted drops in population in Western economies, a labour shortage has been anticipated (Grossman, 2005). With more demand for workers, employers who can design jobs and working environments that meet the personal, family and other non-work needs of employees will have a distinct advantage in winning the war for talent. Statistics demonstrate that Irish birth-rates continue to grow (the Central Statistics Office reported that 60,500 births were registered in Ireland in 2002, the highest birth-rate recorded in 15 years). With more financial pressure to remain in the workforce, young parents are increasingly facing stronger demands on their family and working time. Despite this, IMI research in late 2003 reported that over two-thirds of a survey population indicated that their organisation had no formal work / life balance policy.

In April 2005, the FÁS *Labour Market Commentary* reported that thousands of women returned to the labour force or sought work for the first time. This marks a considerable change in Irish culture where, until relatively recently, females with children were expected to remain in the household and took primary responsibility for raising children. This cultural facet was enshrined in legislation, which until the early 1970s required mothers of children to resign from Civil Service positions, for example. The increased participation of women in the workforce, alongside the continued inflow of migrant workers to Ireland, has served to address labour market tensions, giving Ireland the lowest unemployment rate of any EU economy. Nonetheless, there are still some significant issues around the cost and availability of childcare, particularly in the Dublin area.

An assumption appears to be made often that work / life balance is primarily a concern for female workers and managers. But fatherhood itself has undergone a fundamental change, and young fathers are expected to, and want to, have an equal role in the raising of their children. How many organisations assist these young men in the same way that their female partners are facilitated?

Another assumption made in relation to work / life balance is that it is primarily a concern of people who have young children. McLaughlin & Cullen (2003) unearthed a list of factors that can contribute to work / life imbalance at the levels of the general environment, work and non-work (see **Table 1**).

TABLE 1: FACTORS THAT CAN CONTRIBUTE TO
WORK-LIFE IMBALANCE

Environmental Factors	Work Factors	Non-Work Factors
Economic climate	Downsizing	Additional financial commitments
Transport infrastructure	Workload	Personal interests
Changes in industry / sector	Organisational culture	Children
Government policy	Occupational change	Medical concerns
Legal framework	Work location	Eldercare
Globalisation	Staff turnover	Personal development
National culture	Work / life balance policies / practices	Quality of life
Changing social trends	Promotional opportunities	Changes in personal / family supports

So, what can organisations do to address their employees' work / life balance? McLaughlin & Cullen's research uncovered four main themes for managers, to enable them to help their employees, and their own, work / life balance needs:

- **Understanding:** Managers must be helped to develop a sound understanding of the individual employee's work / life balance needs and to recognise that they change over time. Managers need to see that the provision of work / life balance is not merely 'a nice thing to do' but that it is directly linked to productivity gains and retention of staff.

- **Empowering:** Managers are not adequately trained to facilitate work / life balance initiatives. Training, education and peer communication are central to the development or organisational cultures where work / life balance is valued, and gives value back to the organisation. Organisational productivity is likely to be improved as a result. Managers should be aware of the complexity of work / life balance, but also appreciate its importance, particularly as a strategic retention tool.

- **Developing**: Managers would benefit from planning and reviewing work / life balance plans regularly as work / life balance needs change rapidly. Failure to do this will result in employees leaving to work for competitors who can meet their work / life balance needs better. Managers need to be assisted in providing services, but also in providing information resources and flexible benefits to employees.

- **Facilitating:** Work / life balance initiatives need to be supported by top level management. Such support has to go beyond rhetoric and needs to be valued as a strategic tool for productivity, retention and creating competitive advantage.

The two cases presented here demonstrate how two organisations responded to this very serious, and growing, issue, in a proactive fashion that attempted to embed positive work / life balance policies and practices at the heart of working in the organisation.

References

Cooper, C. (1998). 'The Changing Nature of Work [1]', *Community, Work & Family*, 1(3), pp.313-317.

Dooley, C. (2005). 'Thousands of Women are Returning to Work', *The Irish Times*, Monday, 4 April, p.5.

Grossman, R.J. (2005). 'The Truth about the Coming Labor Shortage', *HR Magazine*, 50(3), pp.46-53.

McLaughlin, A. & Cullen, J. (2003). *Managers & Work / Life Balance: The Case of the Irish Hospitality Industry*. Dublin: IMI / Irish Hotel & Catering Institute.

Milne, J.L. (1999). 'Managers play key role in work / life balance', *The Canadian Manager*, 24(4), p. 5.

O'Connor, M. (2003). *Top Challenges for Managers*, Dublin: IMI.

Peillon, M. (2002). 'Introduction' in Peillon, M. & Corcoran, M.P. (eds), *Ireland Unbound: A Turn of the Century Chronicle*, Dublin: IPA.

Ward, M. & Cullen, J. (2003). *Measuring the Usage and Impact of Work / Life Balance Policies and Programmes: A Survey of Irish Managers*, Dublin: IMI Centre for Management Research.

CASE 8

Balancing the Burden at Trócaire[12]

Trócaire is the official overseas development agency of the Catholic Church in Ireland. It was set up by the Irish Catholic Bishops in 1973 to express the concern of the Irish Church for the suffering of the world's poorest and most oppressed people.

Trócaire has a dual mandate:

- To support long-term development projects overseas and to provide relief during emergencies

- At home, to inform the Irish public about the root causes of poverty and injustice and mobilise the public to bring about global change.

The agency strives to promote human development and social justice in line with Gospel values.

People are Trócaire's key asset and, as such, the organisation believes it is essential to develop and support staff and also to provide a healthy, safe and pleasant place to work. Since it was founded, Trócaire has grown significantly both in terms of income and staff numbers and has also expanded its work in the emergency arena. Increased competition for donor funds had also necessitated the introduction of a major fund-raising appeal at Christmas, which, by its time-bound nature, was a potential source of stress.

---

[12] This case study was prepared with the assistance of Louise Barrett, former Human Resources Officer at Trócaire (2003-2005), and is based on work done in the period 2000-2002.

For Trócaire to remain successful, it became imperative that staff could respond to the changing environment and could deal with additional pressures without becoming stressed. Identifying the level of stress within the organisation, and the specific reasons for the stress, became essential.

With this in mind, management initiated a study on workplace pressures with a particular focus on whether the work environment impacted on employees' ability to maintain a work and home life balance. The Royal College of Surgeons in Ireland (RCSI) was commissioned to carry out this research among staff in 2000. Once the research was completed, the results were studied jointly by management and the union committee and suggested initiatives were implemented.

In 2002, at the suggestion of the union in Trócaire, funds were made available from the Equality Authority (a total budget of €5,000) to conduct follow-up research into work / life balance among its staff. The 'Family Friendly Working Group', made up of staff, union and HR representatives, was set up to oversee the research conducted by Pearn Kandola Occupational Psychologists and the subsequent implementation of findings. Despite its name, the working group was conscious of the need to also look at pressures on staff who were not married or who did not have a family.

The central objectives of the research as defined by HR and management were to:

- Examine levels of job satisfaction and stress experienced by employees of Trócaire.
- Measure level of psychological well-being of employees and coping strategies used to manage pressures in their jobs.
- Provide information that would assist in developing policies and action plans to maximise job satisfaction and deal adequately with the pressures of work in Trócaire.
- Implement recommendations and policies arising out of the research.
- Evaluate the success of the point above.

The key personnel involved in the project were:

- Family Friendly Working Group, comprising staff, management, HR & union representatives.
- RCSI, Department of Psychology.
- Pearn Kandola (Occupational Psychologists).
- Staff – a sample of 79 answered a questionnaire for the RCSI research. A sample of 16 staff participated in, and contributed to, the completion of the Pearn Kandola project *via* questionnaires and focus groups.
- Staff partners / spouses – Three staff members' partners agreed to a telephone interview to assess the impact of work on home life from their perspective in the Pearn Kandola research.

Trócaire's director and management team fully endorsed the project, participated in the research phase and supported the implementation of its recommendations.

The main outcomes were a reading of the stress levels in Trócaire and the implementation of a programme of initiatives and activities to minimise stress as a result of the recommendations received. There is now a greater awareness by both staff and management of the causes and symptoms of stress, how it affects individuals and how it can be minimised.

The main sources of stress identified by the RCSI research programme (2000) included:

- Workload
- Effect of crisis situations on workload (for example, Kosovo, Rwanda)
- Meetings
- Lack of consultation and communication.

The recommendations arising were:

- Improve time management skills
- Improve communication styles (particularly relating to positive feedback, performance review, teamwork)

- Tackle stress effects particular to fund-raising and international departments such as critical incident debriefing, employee assistance programmes, adequate staff resources
- Provide opportunities for time out during overseas trips
- Promotion of physical exercise, importance of developing pastimes and hobbies outside work.

Trócaire immediately set about putting together and implementing a set of initiatives to respond to the research and its recommendations. Individual coaching was made available and a time management course was conducted.

A performance review system was introduced and training provided. An HR manual for overseas-based staff was developed, which specifically includes a section on debriefing. Lunch-time talks and sessions were initiated and encouraged to help increase communication amongst staff. Flexitime was made an option for staff and yoga was made available, with the organisation contributing to some of the cost involved.

The main sources of stress identified in subsequent research by Pearn Kandola in 2003 included:

- Increased workload due to changes in staff and seasonal pressures
- Interpersonal conflict – clash of personalities during a time-bound campaign
- Travel
- Physical work factors, including IT problems
- Crisis situations.

The recommendations arising were:

- To run time management training on a continual basis to help people manage their workload optimally.
- Reduce workload of some staff on ongoing campaigns by fostering a more team-based approach, particularly within emergency campaigns.

- Consideration of the workloads of part-time staff.

- To fully implement a Dignity at Work policy and for people to receive awareness training in this area. It was also recommended to set up a system of designated contact people for individuals to approach if they felt they were in a difficult situation in work.

- Individual debrief when a staff member returns from an overseas trip to ensure that there are no issues arising from the trip that could be a source of stress.

- Provide the option of home-working for the days immediately following a trip overseas as a readjustment period.

- Need to review the current IT system to improve organisational, team and individual efficiencies.

- Promote the existence of the quiet room.[13]

- Since moving to Maynooth, the performance management system was not used as regularly – there was a need to reinvigorate the current system.

Trócaire developed a set of actions based on this further research project and its implementation:

- An in-house time management course was rolled out, which will be repeated at regular intervals.

- A new IT system (Lotus Notes) was implemented in August 2003. The new system includes group meeting software, which will assist in improving people's organisational and time management skills. Remote access was made available in 2004. This has proved invaluable for staff who travel frequently, as they can keep in touch with colleagues and family while travelling.

- The IT platform was reconfigured, with additional servers introduced, thereby reducing the down-time of the computer system.

---

[13] A quiet room is an office space to provide employees with the facility to work quietly without being disturbed.

- The performance management system was redesigned and re-launched in May / June 2003 with a series of workshops and presentations.

- A 'quiet room' was decorated and promoted.

- Yoga sessions have been continued, with Trócaire continuing its contribution to some of the costs of the classes.

- Trócaire has negotiated a reduced rate membership of the Maynooth college gym and other facilities.

- The Dignity at Work policy was agreed with the union. A training programme for this policy was delivered in October 2003.

- The flexitime system was adjusted to give more flexibility to staff, given the longer commute for some staff following the move to Maynooth. It was an agreed way to help minimise the stress faced by commuters.

- The creation of *ad hoc* staff meetings to communicate different work outputs. For example, the Head of Communications & Education held a 20-minute session to explain a new direct mail campaign focusing on the issue of HIV / Aids. At this meeting, the direct mail literature and the reason for addressing HIV / Aids in this manner was explained. Direction was given to staff on where to get supplementary reading on the issue. Staff were advised what to do if they were contacted directly by any reporters about this direct mailing. There was an opportunity for questions and answers.

- The management forum, comprising the management team and staff at Programme Coordinator level (14 in total), has been reactivated and currently meets every six weeks. This group focuses on progress against the Strategic Plan, with special emphasis on organisational objectives, which include Trócaire becoming a Learning Organisation.

- A fortnightly e-zine is produced by the Communications team, providing information on activity in Trócaire.

- All staff are involved in the Strategic Planning Process, which happens every three years. Initially, employees are involved in the planning phase within their own department. Once the plan is finalised, it is rolled out at a staff training day.

- Creation of a working group / task force to look at issues (other than the redundancy negotiation, which was done directly with the union) connected with the move to Maynooth.

- Trócaire again successfully achieved the Excellence Through People (ETP) Award in 2004, for the 6th time in a row. Trócaire was the first and only charity to have been awarded the Excellence Through People standard. Trócaire improved on its overall ETP Audit score as follows: 2002 - 91%; 2003 – 92%; 2004 – 93%. This indicates to staff Trócaire's ongoing and improved commitment to their personal and professional development.

Alignment of "Balancing the Burden" with Trócaire's Overall Business Objectives

In the Strategic Plan 1999-2002, Trócaire's overall business objectives included the following:

- Strategic Objective 5 outlined a commitment to a working environment that is a desirable and happy place to work for all staff, and promotes effective working. This strategic objective's key initiative was to introduce flexible working practices, thereby helping to create the desired working environment that is commitment-orientated and free from workplace stress.

- Strategic Objective 7 stated Trócaire's objective to be a learning organisation, using the initiative of actively seeking feedback. Trócaire, therefore, determined that to create the desired workplace, the organisation needed to understand what possible sources of pressure there were, and what impact this was having on staff, to make changes and learn from the knowledge gained. The management team therefore took the initiative to commission the initial research by RCSI.

The Strategic Plan 2002–2005 included the following business objectives:

- Strategic Objective 1: Relocation – to successfully relocate, minimising the disruption to core functions and re-establishing full capacity. Analysing the possible stress situation and implementing any recommendation made in the research was key to ensuring the smooth move to Maynooth.

- Strategic Objective 6: Progressive HR policies – to help us remain the organisation of choice for current and prospective staff. Again, a work environment that manages possible sources of stress would contribute significantly towards the achievement of this objective.

- Strategic Objective 7: Learning Organisation – to enable Trócaire develop as a learning organisation committed to a culture of innovation. Trócaire is committed to learning from past successes and mistakes and part of that involves researching the organisation from the work / life balance perspective.

The Benefits to the Organisation

In the short term, the "Balancing the Burden" initiative allowed Trócaire not only to identify the level of stress within the organisation but critically, it also enabled us to identify the causes of stress and to seek ways of overcoming these.

Going forward, the challenge for Trócaire is to build on the work completed to date by ensuring that the recommendations from the 2002 report are fully implemented and evaluated. Doing this will ensure that the Trócaire staff remain committed to the organisation and that they enjoy a safe and relatively stress-free work environment.

The initiative has had a positive impact on employees' work and home lives. The information gathered from both sets of research and informal feedback is indicative of the amount of effort Trócaire has put in to ensure staff members have a balance between home and work life. This is achieved through a reduction in potential stressors and the introduction of measures to address residual stressors.

The research has made staff cognisant of the efforts they engage in to minimise work / life imbalances and encouraged them to seek solutions when difficulties arise. The positive impact for staff is best summed up by looking at the results achieved by Trócaire in the "Best Companies to Work for in Ireland" competition 2004. This competition was based on an employee survey. Results were tabulated for approximately 150 participant organisations. Trócaire achieved a Top 10 place overall, and received a special award for Pride in the Workplace.

The Role of Human Resources

The steps taken to ensure the sustainability of the initiative within Trócaire by HR were:

- HR was the key driver behind the initiatives, the collation of data and the implementation and monitoring of most initiatives.
- The establishment of a Family Friendly Working Group.
- The involvement of all major stakeholders in decision making – union, management, staff.
- An increase in members of HR department – creation of new role of HR Officer and the appointment of a full-time manager to take responsibility for HR issues.
- Participation in benchmarking opportunities for our HR work – for example, the "Best Companies to Work for in Ireland" competition.

CASE 9

Flexible Working & Family Friendly
Initiatives at KARE[14]

KARE is an agency that provides services to adults and children with an intellectual disability. It was founded in 1967 by a group of parents and friends and in excess of 400 adults and children with a range of intellectual disabilities in Kildare, East Offaly and West Wicklow avail of its services.

KARE currently employs 205 whole-time equivalent staff. This figure increases to 245 when all staff are counted – including part-time and job sharers. The staff employed by KARE work in a range of different disciplines. These include instructor facilitators, nurses, care assistants, employment officers, social care workers / leaders, co-ordinators, clinicians in occupational therapy, physiotherapy, psychology, social work, speech & language therapy, sports & recreation and clerical / administrative.

The range of services provided includes children's, adult day and residential / respite services. KARE is also patron to two special needs schools: St. Anne's School and St. Mark's School.

KARE's vision is:

> '… that people with a learning disability are seen as equals and take part in society along with everyone else.' (KARE Strategic Plan 2004-2008)

---

[14] This case study was prepared with the assistance of Mary O'Connor, Human Resources Manager at KARE.

It has identified four strategic priorities that will guide the organisation to achieve this vision:

- Becoming more and more person-centred
- Involving families & carers
- Supporting staff
- Building partnerships.

The key driver for the Flexible Working / Family Friendly initiative was the recognition by KARE of the necessity to be flexible in terms of service delivery. The first strategic priority, Person Centredness, requires that service-users are at the centre of everything KARE does and, to do this, KARE needs to be able to respond to their diverse range of changing needs. This requires a great deal of flexibility among staff. However, in order to get real flexibility and commitment from staff, KARE needs to demonstrate *its* commitment to help staff to try to achieve a healthy work / life balance in their lives.

KARE is an independent voluntary organisation with its own board of directors. It receives the majority of its funding from the Health Services Executive and the Department of Education & Science. Because of this, KARE is very limited in terms of its flexibility around pay and conditions, due to being linked to national salary scales and conditions. Flexibility in working arrangements and helping staff to achieve a healthy work / life balance was identified as one area that it could do something about.

Introducing the Flexible Working Initiative

Whilst a certain amount of flexible working was already in operation, it was decided to formalise the situation and, so in 2001, KARE began the process of developing a Flexible Working / Family Friendly Policy for the organisation.

A team was set up to draft a policy and this was then reviewed by the rest of the organisation. The team was made up of representatives from the various different parts of the service.

Following a lot of discussion and review by staff in general, the policy was approved and implemented across the organisation.

A lot of consideration was given to the policy and whether it should outline in detail the circumstances under which a staff member would be granted flexible working arrangements. In the end, it was felt that this might be too restricting and might not always be in the best interest of staff or the organisation. KARE's policy is not prescriptive in terms of what alternative arrangements are possible, thus helping to ensure that it is flexible and does not limit the possibilities. Each application is considered on an individual basis and is always evaluated in terms of its impact on service delivery. Where an application cannot be approved, it is sometimes possible to come up with alternative solutions to the underlying problem that the person faces. These alternatives include transfer to another location, or alternative working hours for a short period of time, to give the staff member an opportunity to make alternative arrangements.

As part of KARE's Operational Plan for 2005, the Flexible Working / Family Friendly policy is due for review and a team is in the process of being set up to do this.

The following are currently in operation under the Flexible Working / Family Friendly initiative:

- Reduced working hours
- Unpaid leave during school holidays, with the facility to have salary spread over twelve months
- Job-sharing
- Secondment
- Leave of absence
- Facility to take parental leave on a part-time basis
- Short-term unpaid leave
- Temporary reduced hours for study purposes
- Time off in lieu.

The Person-Centred planning process is how service-users identify their needs. Sometimes, programmes / activities that they want to get involved in must run outside of the usual working hours of our staff. Whilst a certain amount of flexibility is required as part of employment contracts, staff are more likely to be flexible if they feel that their own needs are recognised by the organisation and will work outside their usual working hours in order to facilitate the needs of particular service-users.

Attracting key staff in the clinical area has proved extremely difficult over the last number of years. Being able to offer flexible working arrangements to potential staff, as part of the recruitment package, has strengthened the ability to attract and retain the right people. A number of these positions were filled on a part-time basis and had this not been done, KARE probably would not have been successful in recruiting people for these positions. There were also a number of situations where there was a danger of losing existing employees and the ability to be able to offer alternative / flexible ways of working helped to retain them.

Where reduced hours or unpaid time off has been approved, it has been possible to assign some of the tasks to other members of staff. An example of this is where two co-ordinators were approved to take unpaid leave during the school holidays in the summer and two other frontline staff temporarily acted as co-ordinators for the period of the leave. This gave them the experience of working at a higher level and fits in with KARE's overall human resource development strategy of giving people opportunities to develop their skills. It also gives the organisation the opportunity to assess them at this level and evaluate their potential in terms of promotion, etc. The money saved because of the co-ordinators' unpaid leave was used to compensate financially the temporary upgrades.

Service-user needs can change, and this sometimes results in different skills being required from staff. If an employee wishes to reduce their hours, there is an opportunity to employ somebody else with the required skills on a part-time basis.

In some cases, the potential impact of a change in working hours can be difficult to assess. Rather than refusing to facilitate the request, it is approved on a temporary basis for a set period of time. This gives all concerned the opportunity to see what the impact is and a decision can then be made on whether the request can be approved on a more permanent basis.

The Role of Human Resources

The Flexible Working / Family Friendly policy is very much aligned to the overall HR strategy within KARE. Supporting staff is one of KARE's four strategic priorities and is based on the attraction, retention and development of flexible, motivated staff. Because of the lack of flexibility in terms of the monetary reward systems / benefits in KARE, the Flexible Working / Family Friendly initiative is a key component of the non-monetary benefits package in KARE.

The role of HR in the process is very much one of supporting line management to meet service requirements, whilst at the same time helping to ensure a good work / life balance for staff. Any flexible working arrangements must take place within the agreed staffing levels and HR ensures that the employment ceiling is not exceeded. HR also acts in a co-ordinating role to help ensure that all applications for flexible working arrangements are consistently and fairly evaluated and that all factors are taken into consideration prior to reaching a decision on whether the request can be facilitated.

Benefits to KARE

The benefits of having such a policy include:

- A more person-centred approach to service delivery
- Improved flexibility in service delivery
- Helping to attract and retain key staff
- Helping to promote a more positive working environment where staff feel valued

- Providing opportunities for staff development
- Reducing non-attendance.

The above information was provided through:

- Feedback from service-users, parents, families, etc on service delivery
- Feedback from staff
- Performance Management
- Induction
- Exit interviews
- Team meetings.

A staff survey has been developed and is due to be carried out in 2005. It will include formal feedback from staff on how they feel the flexible working arrangement policy contributes to supporting staff. Informal feedback received from staff to date indicates that they feel valued and more motivated because KARE tries to facilitate their requests, where possible. In cases where it is not possible to do this, the staff members in question can understand the reason why the request is not approved. This has led to an increased sense of loyalty by staff, and thus they are less likely to leave or go out on sick leave.

The following are a selection of comments, both from a staff and a management perspective, regarding the Flexible Working / Family Friendly initiative in KARE:

> "KARE's Family Friendly policy has allowed me to continue to develop my career, whilst also being able to fulfil my responsibilities to my family. Had I not been able to reduce my hours to match school hours, I would have had to seriously consider resigning from my job."

> "The Family Friendly policy gave me the opportunity to negotiate different working arrangements with one of my most valued staff, for whom the juggle of home

and work commitments had become a major source of stress. Her working 10 hours less a week did not significantly impact on her caseload but certainly made her a much more content and motivated person."

"Getting suitably qualified nurses is getting more and more difficult. Having some flexibility around hours and working arrangements has helped in the recruitment of these grades."

"Being able to take unpaid leave during the school summer holidays has reduced the stress of making alternative childminding arrangements and has allowed me spend more time with my family."

"Being able to take parental leave on a part-time basis after my baby was born encouraged me to stay with KARE. Had I not been able to do this, I would have considered looking around for a part-time job."

"By being able to reduce my working hours, I was able to complete a part-time course and get a recognised qualification, without having to give up my job."

"It is great being able to take time off in lieu of extra time worked – it is like having more holidays."

"It was great to get the opportunity to work at the next level. It gave me a better of understanding of what the role involves and I would be much more confident in applying for a similar position if one was to become available."

Summary

Overall, the flexible working arrangements policy within KARE has been successful. However, sometimes when an initiative like this is introduced into an organisation, there is a danger that it becomes the norm and staff see it as an entitlement rather than a perk. This can result in a negative impact on service delivery. As an organisation, KARE is aware of the need to assess needs within the organisation continually to ensure that the balance between service delivery and supporting staff is maintained. An initiative like this requires a partnership or team approach, if it is to be successful and the needs of the service-users needs to be central to any decision made around flexible working.

6

DIVERSITY

One of the effects of the recent economic boom period in Ireland was that we rapidly changed from being a largely mono-cultural society with a tradition of emigration. Over the past 20 years, the configuration of Ireland's labour market has changed to the extent that we are now a full employment economy, with some two million people currently at work.

The accession of 10 new states to the EU in May 2004 has resulted in much greater numbers of foreign workers eligible to come to work legally in Ireland. Net immigration to Ireland is currently running at higher levels than ever before. It has been estimated that around 30% of immigrants to Ireland are returning Irish nationals, many of whom have been abroad for over 10 years. Figures from the Department of Social & Family Affairs report the numbers of people from the 10 new EU states who came to Ireland up to February 2005 (see **Table 2**). These immigrants are perceived by business as essential human resources, who have done much to ease the labour market shortages experienced at the height of the boom years. Many have established businesses themselves to meet the needs of the new communities such as pubs, restaurants, retail outlets and media, but the majority of newcomers to Ireland are working in established Irish businesses.

TABLE 2: IMMIGRATION TO IRELAND FROM 10 ACCESSION STATES (MAY 2004 - FEBRUARY 2005)

Country	Total
Poland	32,648
Lithuania	14,700
Latvia	7,519
Slovakia	5,830
Czech Republic	3,755
Hungary	2,213
Estonia	1,952
Malta	148
Slovenia	75
Cyprus	28

With members of some 160 different nationalities living in Ireland, understanding the national cultural identity of new employees has only recently presented as a challenge to managers accustomed to working in a mono-cultural environment.

> 'Diversity management acknowledges that there are distinct business advantages for employers who value the social and cultural heterogeneity of their workforce by recognising, utilising and valuing differences that exist in any one group of employees. It has evolved from past programmes such as Affirmative Action (AA) and Equal Employment Opportunity (EEO).' (Talbot & Cullen, 2004)

Diversity is a highly complex issue and it is important not to limit the understanding of it solely to cultural issues. The Employment Equality Act, 1998 introduced nine categories by which it is illegal to discriminate: race, gender, disability, family status, age, sexual orientation, marital status, religious belief or membership of the travelling community.

Diversity management is not about trying to control how heterogeneity impacts on a workplace. Rather it is about embracing the range of backgrounds that exist in a workforce in order that the organisation can learn and improve from the experience of its multifaceted workforce. It is also about recognising the reality that many of those workers, newly-arrived to Ireland, face. Many are working at jobs for which they are over-qualified, while they are improving their language skills. Writing in *The Irish Times* on newly-arrived immigrants, Kate Holmquist points out:

> 'The fact that such a large proportion of the workforce is working below its potential is stunting our overall economic growth, the Economic & Social Research Institute (ESRI) warned in its latest quarterly forecast. It ranked Ireland 15th in terms of quality of life but we could have been far higher up the ladder... Migrants contributed 0.4 per cent to GNP per head. If these people had been used to their full potential, GNP per head would have risen to 1 per cent gross GNP per head in the five years to 2003, which would have had benefits for the wider economy.'

Strategic diversity management uses the skills, qualifications and competencies of individuals who are not from a 'traditional' Irish background (a concept which in itself will undoubtedly become irrelevant), to contribute to an organisation's competitive position.

The case presented here is the widely-celebrated Equality & Diversity initiative at Dublin Bus, which represents a genuine, and successful attempt, to address gender imbalance and the growing cultural diversity within the organisation.

References

Holmquist, K. (2005). 'Eastern Promise', *The Irish Times*, Monday, 4 April, p.17.

Talbot, J. & Cullen, J. (2004). *Understanding Diversity Management in Ireland: A Survey of Management Practices,* Dublin: IMI Centre for Management Research.

CASE 10

Dublin Bus' Equality & Diversity Programme[15]

Dublin Bus (Bus Átha Cliath) is a major semi-state public transport provider in the City of Dublin and its environs. The service operates 1,062 buses on 200 routes and carries approximately 500,000 passengers each day. The company employs approximately 3,400 people, and like most transport companies, traditionally was male-dominated.

The Equality & Diversity Programme was established in Dublin Bus in January 2001. It was an initiative by the Manager, Human Resources, in response to a number of emerging concerns, including the low percentage of women in the workplace and a low representation of women in certain grades in the organisation. Representation of women in bus-driving grades was affected by the fact that women often left work because the demands of the rosters conflicted with their child-care needs.

Change had occurred in the age profile of employees and there were changes occurring in terms of family and work / life balance needs, and needs in relation to people with disabilities. There was also dramatic change in the cultural diversity of the workforce, which now employs people from 50 different countries of origin. Management was also aware of its legal obligations, as an employer and as a service-provider, in relation to equality legislation.

The programme was established to develop a culture where equality and diversity are established as core values within the organisation. It acknowledges that, to deliver a quality customer

---

[15] This case study was prepared with the assistance of Patricia Normanly, Equality & Diversity Officer at Dublin Bus.

service, Dublin Bus is committed to creating a fair and truly inclusive workplace, where individual differences are respected and where all staff are enable to do their best work.

> 'We believe that the principles of equality and inclusion enhance the efficiency and fulfilment of our employees, empower us to meet the changing needs of our customers, and connect us to the community that we serve.' (Joe Meagher, Managing Director, Dublin Bus, 2005)

Dublin Bus acknowledges that the workforce and customer-base are made up of people of many differences. By acknowledging and valuing these differences, the organisation can ensure a working environment where people feel valued and where their potential is fully realised. This, in turn, Dublin Bus believes, will help to provide a better and safer service for customers, improve staff morale, reduce absenteeism and facilitate good teamwork. It aims to create an environment of equality, dignity and respect and to put in place procedures throughout the organisation to ensure best practice in all business functions.

Introduction

An Equality & Diversity Officer was appointed in January 2001, with the role of 'establishing and developing an equality and diversity programme'. The Equality & Diversity Officer reports directly to the Manager, Human Resources. From the outset, there was commitment from senior management to the integration of equality and diversity policies into all aspects of the business.

> '... there is commitment from our Board, from myself and from our management team ... with the intention of embedding this work into all aspects of Dublin Bus and integrating it into our mainstream everyday

business.' (Alan Westwell, Managing Director, Dublin Bus, 2002)

This commitment was essential as a starting point and also at the different stages of the development of the programme.

A working group was established, made up of representatives of staff at various grades and locations. This group played a key role in the Equality Review, which was carried out from 2001 to 2002. The review involved a number of stages, including the collection and collation of statistical information in relation to the workforce – for example, gender, grade, age, years of service, country of origin, etc., as well as the review of policies and procedures in recruitment, career development, training, promotion, work arrangements and conditions, grievance handling and publicity.

Focus groups and interviews were conducted with members of staff from all areas of the organisation. The final stage involved drawing up recommendations and an action plan.

Equality & Diversity Action Plan 2003 - 2010

The Action Plan sets out three key objectives, which are the focus of the Equality & Diversity Programme for the period 2003 – 2010. The objectives are:

- Supporting and Protecting Staff and Business Needs.
- Building Competencies and Awareness.
- Facilitating and Driving Change.

By setting goals within a timeframe, issues that arise from the Equality Review are translated into practical action. Under each of the objectives, a number of practical steps have been set out that can be achieved in developing best practice within a timeframe. They include:

- Policies on Equality & Diversity, Dignity & Respect, Equal Status, Recruitment & Selection and Work / Life Balance.

- Supports & Structures.
- Raising Awareness.
- Positive People Management.
- Inclusion, Participation and Partnership.
- Monitoring and Evaluation.

Some of these areas were being worked on while the review was being conducted, others are in progress and some have yet to be developed.

The Action Plan places an emphasis on participation and is committed to partnership and consultation through joint groups of staff members, trade union representatives and management representatives, working on specific issues.

The Plan also includes a commitment to monitoring and evaluation to ensure the on-going development of an equality infrastructure in Dublin Bus. Monitoring includes data collection and analysis on a regular basis, progress reports, and identification of potential blocks to equality and development of measures of action to overcome such inequalities. It also includes a review of the programme.

Data is analysed on an annual basis. While data shows that there is a low percentage of women in the organisation and low percentage of women coming into the organisation, the annual analysis of data also looks at, not just the percentage of women in the organisation, but, more importantly, where women are working in the organisation, and monitors their progression. The analysis drawn from such data gives an indication of progress and informs the development of future actions.

Business Case & Key Objectives

At the outset, the programme identified short-term and long-term objectives.

The business case for some of the short-term objectives were related to equality legislation and the company's obligations and potential claims under that legislation – for example, to:

- Establish and implement a policy in relation to Dignity & Respect at Work and the Prevention of Bullying & Harassment
- Establish and implement a policy in relation to Equality & Diversity and the promotion of equal opportunity.
- Establish and implement a policy in relation to cultural diversity and the promotion of anti-racism in the workplace
- Design and deliver awareness training for all staff and specific training for managers and supervisors.

The long-term objectives go beyond compliance and are strongly linked to a business case, which acknowledges that certain initiatives can improve efficiency, recruitment, and employee retention and customer relations – for example:

- Integrate the Action Plan within all business functions.
- Ensure adherence to best practice in equality in all organisational activities.
- Ensure participation and inclusion of all stakeholders.
- Develop structures for data collection, and analysis of such data, as an indicator of progress and for development of future actions.
- Provide information, challenge stereotyping and foster teamwork and inclusiveness in all organisational activities.

These objectives have been achieved as follows:

- **Values & Good Practice within the Company:** The development of a strong and relevant set of values encourages the creativity of staff, attracts and retains good staff, and assists managers in dealing with change, thus ensuring quality work practices and a sustained focus on the long-term goals of the business.
- **Company Image:** Investment in equality and diversity has enhanced the public image and the Company is now perceived as a more progressive employer, one that is in touch with the demands of the workforce, the supplier and the customers.

- **Impact on HR Function:** The programme has enhanced the HR function in a number of ways, including facilitating the review of HR procedures and practices – for example, the redesign of application forms; training of interview panels; development of guidelines for managers and supervisors; specific analysis of data in relation to workforce; additional support for staff and managers, favourable publicity for HR.

Lessons Learned

Lessons learned to date include:

- **Integration in all aspects of the business:** Since the programme was established, it has already shown that, while issues of equality and diversity are primarily associated with equal opportunity for employees and equal treatment of customers, it is also about acknowledging and valuing difference and capturing the benefits of diversity in all aspects of the business. Rather than being an added responsibility or just about compliance with legislation, it is about best practice in all aspects of our relationship with the people employed and the communities served. It is part of the management of change in a changing workplace, a changing city, a changing nation and a changing Europe.

- **Planned and systematic approach**: If equality and diversity is to be integrated in overall business of the organisation, it must be implemented in a planned and systematic way. This will ensure that key objectives can be set out, that timeframes can be established, that measurement structures and communication structures can be put in place, and that the programme can be evaluated and reviewed as to its effectiveness.

- **Policies and procedures:** Policies and procedures need to be developed in relation to equality and diversity issues, they need to be effectively communicated to staff on an on-going basis and need to be supported by on-going relevant training for staff, managers and supervisors. Training should raise awareness of the various issues and provide education in relation to practical implementation of policies and procedures.

- **Partnership and consultation:** Everybody in the workplace has a responsibility for ensuring that the programme is effective. Inclusion, consultation and participation can often appear difficult to organise, slow to work with and bring its own problems but, Dublin Bus has learned that, in the long term, it is the only way to bring out effective change. At the end of the day, it has enormous benefits in terms of awareness-raising and buy-in at all levels in the organisation.

- **Networks and supports:** It is essential for those involved in the implementation of equality and diversity programmes to form links with similar organisations that are involved in this process in order to share best practice and benchmark initiatives. It is also essential that links be formed with agencies, organisations and Government Departments, who offer support and guidance in relation to the various areas to be addressed.

- **Commitment:** The commitment of senior management needs to be visible, active and ongoing. This commitment needs to be communicated to all staff and, in particular, those with responsibility for the management of staff and direct delivery of services. This commitment can be maintained by keeping managers and staff involved in the process, regular communication, briefings, and celebrating and re-enforcing achievements.

Challenges

The challenges for the future are:

- Ensuring that commitment is maintained throughout the organisation, particularly, in the face of change both internally and externally

- Reviewing policies, procedures, and practices and how they are being implemented

- Maintaining a strong consultative approach by ensuring that changing needs can be expressed and addressed
- Measuring progress constantly, as well as cost / benefit analysis and addressing areas of concern
- Communicating and reinforcing best practice throughout the organisation
- Creating employment opportunities and transport services for the entire community, including those who experience inequalities
- Achieving a workplace where under-represented groups have access and can progress.

In a changing environment, the focus of the organisation must continue to be on the changing needs of staff and customers and initiatives must be developed constantly to keep pace with these changes. In order to survive, Dublin Bus needs to be receptive to change and innovation and this means developing strategies to ensure that the workplace is one where:

- The diversity of the general population is reflected in the workforce and the strengths of this diversity can contribute to the effectiveness of the service and the success of the organisation
- Structures of partnership and consultation are developed to ensure that more people, especially those whose voice is often not heard, are included in dialogue, planning and decision-making, so that a broad spectrum of knowledge and experience can be positively used in the organisation
- Everybody in the organisation is aware of their role in relation to the equality and diversity values of the organisation, and those values are incorporated into best practice across the various functions in the organisation
- Fairness, respect and inclusion are demonstrated in all aspects of relationships with employees and potential employees, customers, suppliers and the communities served by the business.

7
INNOVATION

The relatively recent turnaround of Ireland's economic fortunes was based on a number of factors which aimed to encourage foreign-direct investment from large multinational companies. It has long been recognised that the ingredients which led to the boom years of the late 1990s (such as our large labour supply, a competitive Corporation Tax rate, our location, education system and English-speaking people) is now being replicated by lower-cost economies. Ireland has witnessed what is quite possibly the first round of layoffs in traditional manufacturing over the past 18 months or so. Sustaining economic prosperity will require a new set of requirements which, in short, will mean reconfiguring our business culture going forward. The key words for the coming decade for Irish business will be 'innovate' and 'internationalise'. Increased focus will be placed on R&D functions, and indigenous Irish companies of all sizes will be urged to place research and creativity at the top of their agendas. Enterprise Ireland's chief executive, Frank Ryan, has recently been quoted as saying that:

> 'We want to see an R&D department in every company in our portfolio. We want an R&D department to be as common in an Irish company as a recruitment department.' (Kennedy, 2005)

Innovation is provided by encouraging productive imagination at all levels of corporate cultures. Charles Leadbeater (2003) has written:

'Innovation is no longer the preserve of men in white coats and experts. The capacity for innovation is widely distributed across society and consumers expect to have their say in the process' (p.190).

For companies to be innovative, inventiveness will have to be front-and-centre at all levels of Irish organisations, regardless of their size or function. Many of today's successful Irish companies have long recognised this and fought against the 'established wisdom' that told them their service, model or approach wouldn't work. They believed otherwise and proved the nay-sayers wrong. Perhaps the most famous example of this is Ryanair, but there are numerous other examples of Irish SMEs that regularly think outside the box. It's interesting that many of these are companies where creativity is their *raison d'être*. Small animation houses, such as Brown Bag Films, have achieved international recognition for their work and now produce a slate of projects in Europe and the Middle East. Brown Bag was born at a time when Dublin's animation sector had experienced a significant downturn and the major foreign companies had closed their Irish operations. Its success is indicative of the need to be innovative when the traditional models fail (Cullen, 2005). There is a sense that innovation happens more easily in these companies, because their business is creativity. It would be wrong, however, to assume that innovation cannot happen in larger established firms. The challenge is to ensure that it doesn't get lost or thrown aside by existing cultural or structural constraints in organisational settings.

On a daily basis, HR managers deal with situations that require innovative thinking in relation to problems at an organisational and a personal level. Peter Drucker's maxim that the only constant is change might be paraphrased that the only constant for HR managers in the future will be innovation.

Case 11 in this collection demonstrates AXA Ireland's recognition that innovation happens at different centres of creativity in an organisation and describes a set of programmes

that have been highly successful in involving all employees in delivering customer-focused innovation. The results have been excellent for the organisation, with one initiative alone saving the company €500k in its first year.

The final case chosen for this collection could, like many of the other cases, have appeared under any of the other chapter headings. It encapsulates profound organisational cultural change, innovative use of technologies, organisational learning and work / life balance. The Public Appointments Service story since the start of the millennium is one of constant innovation, which has resulted in a virtually new organisation over a very short period of time. This rapid process of change and evolution was dictated by market demands, to which innovative responses were required from its managers, employees at all levels, and from its multifaceted client-base.

References

Cullen, J. (2005). 'Brown Bag' case in Johnson, G., Scholes, K. & Whittington, R. (eds), *Exploring Corporate Strategy: Texts & Cases*, 7th Edition, Harlow: FT Prentice Hall.

Kennedy, J. (2005). 'Innovation is Key for Irish SMEs', *Irish Independent* 'Digital Ireland' supplement, p.1.

Leadbeater, C. (2003). *Up the Down Escalator: Why the Global Pessimists Are Wrong*, London: Penguin.

CASE 11

AXA Ireland – Involving, Innovating, Achieving[16]

The AXA Ireland Innovations Department, in conjunction with Human Resource Department, have developed and implemented unique, comprehensive and integrated programmes to drive and manage innovation activity within the business. The programmes are designed to involve each and every employee in AXA in customer-focused innovation. They are measurable programmes of change that are delivering results for the bottom line. Since their introduction in early 2000, the programmes have been hugely successful. In less than five years, they have delivered 5,000 customer-focused business improvement ideas – 3,000 of which already have been implemented. In addition, the programmes have contributed more than €1.5m *per annum* to profitability and have enabled AXA leverage from global synergy. They have also delivered individual and organisational learning and development and cultural transformation.

AXA Ireland is a leading motor insurer in the Irish market. It distributes its products through a network of branch offices, insurance brokers and telesales operations. Formerly known as the Guardian PMPA Group, the company was acquired in 1999 by AXA, the largest insurance company in the world, with 130,000 employees.

Although AXA Ireland has a very experienced staff, in the past, staff had limited involvement in business improvement. A staff attitude survey conducted in 1999 revealed morale problems. This translated into poor customer service delivery and problems in

---

[16] This case study was prepared with the assistance of Catherine Whelan, Programme Manager at AXA Ireland.

implementing business improvement and change. In addition, market inflationary pressures had impacted negatively on business results.

In 1999, a new CEO, John O'Neill, was appointed with a clear strategy for delivering a strong brand, a motivated and participative workforce, a customer-focused culture, a change-enabled business and a return to profitability. A critical part of his strategy involved delivering the new AXA brand to the market supported by unique product offerings, competitive prices, exemplary service and a fully-engaged staff. To develop the business and deliver profitability, AXA needed to become better and faster at implementing product innovation and customer-focused change. This vision presented a substantial challenge for the Innovations Department and the Human Resources team.

To achieve the business turnaround required a HR strategy that would move staff from a passive to an active role in brand development, customer service delivery and business improvement that was clearly linked to bottom-line results. This would involve making all employees at every level, both responsible and accountable for delivering innovation and continuous improvement as part of their daily jobs.

To achieve this, AXA had to deliver measurable programmes of change that:

- Defined the innovation activity
- Were engaging
- Maximised employee participation
- Delivered innovation
- Focused on implementation
- Delivered cultural transformation, organisational learning, growth and development – and most importantly, programmes that would deliver for the customer, the employee and AXA.

In early 2000, AXA Ireland Innovations Department, in conjunction with the HR team, embarked on a five-step strategy to engage employees and to develop the innovation capability of the business. This strategy involved defining, engaging, managing, integrating, communicating and measuring employee engagement and innovation results. The five steps are detailed below:

1. Defining the meaning of Innovation in the AXA Ireland Business

The first step involved defining the meaning of innovation for the AXA Ireland business. This was a critical step, in terms of raising awareness among staff and creating understanding. It was also important in terms of leveraging from global synergy by encouraging the concept of idea re-use. To clarify the meaning of innovation in the business, AXA Ireland developed the Innovation Quadrant, which separates innovation into four distinct activities:

1. Create (new business opportunities)
2. Improve (existing products and processes)
3. Eliminate (non-value adding activities)
4. Re-use (global success stories).

The Innovation Quadrant was a tool that employees could use every day to generate ideas from their daily interaction with external and internal customers and processes.

2. Delivering comprehensive Innovation Programmes to empower staff to achieve change

The second step involved developing comprehensive Innovation Programmes that empowered employees to achieve change. Two innovation programmes were introduced. The first focused on employees delivering substantial business improvement projects through team-based innovation. The second innovation programme empowered staff to achieve customer-focused innovation and continuous improvement as part of their daily jobs – focusing on *simple improvements* that could be implemented *quickly* and at *little cost*.

Both programmes are comprehensive frameworks that encourage staff to seek actively the views of their customers. Employees are also encouraged to view themselves and their colleagues as customers of the AXA business – and to consider the service they both give and receive on a daily basis.

The AXA Ireland innovation programmes manage the innovation activity from idea concept through to implementation. They also provide opportunities for employees to grow, learn and develop as part of the process.

3. Integrating the Innovation activity with business systems and processes – to drive ownership, idea implementation and cultural change

To sustain the innovation effort, drive implementation and achieve cultural change, the third step involved operationalising the innovation activity. The innovation programmes are linked to the strategic planning and IT processes. They are also fully integrated with HR programmes – for example, the performance management system.

Each employee in AXA now has a customer-focused innovation objective – it is one of five objectives linked to pay. For the majority of employees, the objective involves implementing one simple business improvement idea during the course of the 12-month performance management cycle. The innovation objective can be achieved through individual or team-based effort. A clear linkage has also been created between successful participation in the innovation programmes and career progression within the business.

This has represented a substantial change in the role of AXA employees – as they are now required to deliver customer-focused innovation as part of their daily job – and are rewarded on this basis.

4. Supporting the Innovation effort with a Comprehensive Communication Strategy

The fourth step in developing AXA's innovation capability required the Innovations & HR teams to support the initiative with a comprehensive communication strategy, to reinforce the innovation message to all staff daily. This is achieved through development of a specific innovation brand, screensavers, intranet, magazines, and story-telling, including customer and employee testimony.

In addition, the communication strategy involved developing and implementing employee recognition structures. This resulted in the establishment of quarterly and annual innovation award ceremonies. The awards recognise employee achievements in the areas of idea generation, implementation, project management, learning and successful re-use. In addition, the awards enable AXA to create role models within the business.

To further strengthen the communication strategy, an innovation corridor was established. This is the corridor on the way to the staff restaurant which is visited by most staff daily. This space is used to house innovation initiatives, share learning, and communicate both team and individual achievements.

5. Measuring the results, driving accountability and creating a clear linkage between the innovation activity and profitability

The Innovations & HR teams took the view that the employee engagement strategy must be quantifiable and capable of being directly linked to achievement and financial results. This was viewed as critical in terms of gaining business buy-in for the initiative. Therefore, the fifth step was to build a system of measurement that would enable AXA to drive accountability, track employee participation and innovation progress and results.

This was achieved through the creation of an innovation database. All employees in AXA must register their ideas on the innovation database. They must also record the idea's progress, idea approvals achieved, and conduct a cost / benefit analysis as part of their performance objectives.

The innovation database is used in AXA to share the knowledge generated and to measure innovation results. Reports on innovation progress are issued regularly on a departmental, team and individual basis. Reports are distributed throughout the business and focus on driving *idea implementation*. The reports are also used to measure how well teams and individuals are progressing with their innovation objective and whether further assistance or support is required. In addition, the reports enable AXA to measure employee innovation achievements and award the appropriate bonus payment. The reports form an important part of the overall communication strategy.

The innovation database has enabled AXA Ireland to measure employee participation, idea generation, progress and costs and benefits. It has also enabled AXA to measure and track innovation performance at an organisational, departmental and individual level. This has helped AXA drive *responsibility* and *accountability* for innovation management to all levels of the business.

In addition, the database and reporting system has enabled AXA Ireland to create a clear linkage between employee participation, innovation activity and profitability.

Summary

The AXA Ireland Innovation Programmes represent a unique and integrated approach to achieving business turnaround through innovation management. The programmes have enabled AXA to tap into a previously under-used resource – employees' knowledge – in the interest of the customer and the business. The programmes are clearly linked to AXA strategy and are measurable programmes of change that have delivered substantial benefits for the customer, the employee and AXA.

AXA Ireland Innovation Programmes delivered:

Results for the Customer

- Since the programmes' introduction, AXA Ireland has achieved a 20-point improvement in the Customer Satisfaction index, which is significant. The majority of AXA customers now sit within the 'highly retained' category.

- This HR initiative enabled AXA to launch a unique product offering to the market. This new product incorporates the use of mobile and satellite technology to monitor driving speeds, enabling AXA to deliver competitive rates for young male drivers. AXA continues to investigate opportunities to use technological advances in product development – to deliver for the customer, and to achieve market differentiation and competitive advantage.

- As a result of employee innovation, a substantial number of products and processes have been improved. In addition, non-value-adding activities have been identified and eliminated. For instance, AXA has removed the requirement for new business customers to complete a proposal form. New business transactions are now completed over the phone. This saves time and money for customers and for AXA. It also enables employees to improve the quality of their own work and working environment.

- AXA has extended the Innovation Programmes to incorporate its key business partners. A new Broker Partner Innovation Award Programme was also developed and launched to the intermediary network with tremendous success. There is greater potential to tap into knowledge networks that exists through partnerships that can help build the AXA business going forward.

Results for the Employee

- Over the past five years, an average 80% of staff implemented a customer-focused business improvement idea and achieved their innovation objective and bonus payment under the annual performance management programme.

- More than 50% of staff achieved special recognition awards for both team-based and individual innovation initiatives.

- Since this initiative was introduced, AXA Ireland has ranked among the five top AXA companies in the world for its performance in terms of Employee Satisfaction. The highest-scoring dimensions of this survey relate to employee participation and idea management. In addition, the focus AXA has on clients is also ranked highly. The overall scores have risen by 31 points, representing a significant achievement.

- AXA Ireland employees continue to grow, learn and develop as part of their involvement in ongoing business improvement. HR programmes continue to develop employee participation methodologies and to link them to strategic imperatives on customer servicing, cost management and profitability.

Results for AXA

- Since the programmes' introduction, 5,000 customer-focused business improvement ideas have been generated.

- 3,000 of the good ideas generated already have been implemented.

- This year, one idea alone delivered a saving of €500k.

- This programme has enabled AXA to improve productivity through employee engagement. In addition, linking the innovation objective to pay and idea implementation enabled AXA to deliver a self-financing Performance Management system. The innovation achievements offset the full cost of the Performance Management system in its first year of operation.

- The AXA Innovation Programmes actively promote the concept of idea re-use. As a result, a number of global success stories have been re-used in AXA Ireland. The AXA Ireland intranet site is an example of re-use. Leveraging from global synergy is a low risk, cost-effective way of achieving innovation. In addition, the AXA Ireland Innovation Programmes represent a re-use opportunity for the AXA Group worldwide.

- The Innovation Programmes are enabling AXA to 'listen to customers' by engaging employees, key partners and customers in developing the business.

- AXA Ireland returned to profitability in 2002 and is moving from strength to strength – it is now one of the most profitable companies in the AXA World. This programme continues to develop and contribute in customer, employee and financial terms.

Delivering Innovation in AXA Ireland – a unique approach

The AXA Ireland approach to innovation management is unique. Cranfield University, the number one provider of executive education in the UK, has published a series of papers on the AXA Ireland Innovation experience – the AXA case study is being used by Cranfield on its Executive MBA programme. In addition, Cranfield has submitted the case study to a clearing-house for use by universities worldwide, as it is considered 'new learning' in the area of innovation and human resource management.

CASE 12

The Public Appointments Service[17]

In October 2004, the Office of the Civil Service & Local Appointments Commission changed its name to the Public Appointments Service. This change was far from cosmetic and was underpinned by a preceding five-year period of significant innovation and change. The Public Appointments Service retained the traditional ideals of probity, fairness and impartiality in the public service recruitment system, but incorporated a high degree of flexibility to meet the needs of a recruitment market that had altered radically over the years of the Celtic Tiger boom.

The bedrock of the Office of the Civil Service & Local Appointments Commission has always been transparency, and a very strong reputation for this has been retained since the foundation of the State. In an effort to ensure that public sector employment could not show any form of favouritism, a recruitment system emerged over the years that ended up becoming bound up in extensive red tape, overtly bureaucratic and heavily dependant on rules and regulations. While existing to protect the underlying ethos of the public service, these rules eventually were to become barriers, at a time when changes in Irish society demanded an increasingly responsive service to marketplace demands.

Both internal and external factors drove the need for greater levels of innovation in the Public Appointments Service. During the years of the Celtic Tiger, competition for skilled candidates grew from the private sector. Coupled with huge labour market

---

17   This case study was prepared with the assistance of Martin Bourke, Head of Corporate Affairs at the Public Appointments Service.

tensions during this period, internal processes were impeding the recruitment of necessary candidates.

Five years ago, Bryan Andrews was appointed CEO. An experienced senior civil servant in the Department of Social, Community & Family Affairs, he understood too well the frustrations with the system and, alongside staff members of the organisation, sought to find a better way. Central to the new CEO's philosophy was that, in order to provide excellent customer service, you first had to attempt to understand the clients' needs. During the early stages of the organisation's transformation programme, questions were asked as to who the organisation's clients actually were. This led to an increased focus on the needs of Secretaries General (Civil Service), County Managers (Local Authorities) and Chief Executives (Health Service), while continuing to recognise the level of service required at the candidate level. The Public Appointments Service faced the challenge of getting the clients' needs, opinions and frustrations to the core of the organisation. To achieve this, a customer relations management unit was established. All clients were given a single point of contact in the Public Appointments Service. Following this, the next step was to ensure that the concept of service and relationship management was not the sole preserve of one specific unit in the organisation. Through the restructuring of staff and the redefining of roles, particularly at middle management level, everybody in the organisation was placed in a situation where they were facing the customer. What emerged was an ongoing, rolling programme of customer relationship initiatives throughout the Public Appointments Service. Through weekly meetings with clients, frequent newsletters, customer panels and surveys, the channel of communication with the client was well-established and widened.

It had long been conceived that a 'drop-in' testing centre be developed to enable a more efficient running of the testing of candidates for vacancies. During the foot-and-mouth disease scare some five years ago, it became difficult to bring large numbers of people to major centres for testing. This highlighted the need to bring people to test centres in smaller numbers and thus presented the organisation with its opportunity to develop its 'drop-in' centre. The organisation devised the concept of the 'SMART Centre', which aimed to test smaller numbers of candidates in a more efficient manner. Central to the thinking around the 'SMART Centre' was a critical examination of all aspects of the testing process, with a view to reducing significantly the cycle time it took to attract, test and recruit candidates to the public services.

Previously, vacancies for positions in the civil service were advertised and, usually, thousands of applications were received. Competitions ran some weeks later, by which time a significant fall-off in attendees would have occurred. People successful in the competition were then invited to attend an interview, usually some weeks later, by which time, another group of potential employees would have found alternative employment. The 'SMART Centre' concept was to rapidly improve turnaround times and significantly reduce fall-off in numbers between each stage.

Prior to this, the turnaround time from application to employment could have been up to eight or nine months; with the introduction of the 'SMART Centre', this was reduced to days. The newly-devised system allowed candidates come to the Centre and be tested in the morning. Results were available in the afternoon and demands for staff from client departments were matched against successful candidates, which meant that assignment to vacancies could happen very quickly. Public Appointments Service staff applied business process re-engineering techniques to identify any unnecessary loops in the process. The result was the dramatic increase in the speed of service to clients and a corresponding increase in service satisfaction levels from candidates.

The use of emerging Internet technologies added further to the level of innovation being deployed by the Public Appointments Service. Over the last five years, the organisation has invested heavily in e-recruitment initiatives. The most significant output from this investment has been the development of the organisation's interactive website: www.publicjobs.ie. It is interesting to note that, such was the public reaction to this website, the organisation began to be identified with publicjobs.ie and, in many cases, this came to be perceived as the name of the organisation!

The functionality of the website has been developed systematically over the last few years. Through publicjobs.ie, candidates can apply for all jobs advertised by the Public Appointments Service. The system allows them to submit applications, update CVs and express an interest in jobs that may not yet be advertised. Through a two-way messaging system, candidates are kept up-to-date on progress on campaigns and results. Shortly, candidates will be able to book slots at testing centres and to identify interview slots to suit their travel needs, while client organisations will be able to track the progress of their campaigns and view real-time information on the level of applications being received.

The web-based initiative has proved to be very successful and the majority of applications received by the Public Appointments Service are now received online. For example, well in excess of 90% of applications (nearly 10,000) for the most recent Garda recruitment drive were received online. The use of such web-based technology has had major benefits for the staff of the organisation. Campaigns can now be processed significantly faster, while, at the same time, removing a large amount of monotonous processing from the system.

Despite the huge success of publicjobs.ie, the Public Appointments Service continues to provide multiple channels through which people can opt to come through the organisation. Those candidates with disabilities, people without access to web technology and people with other particular needs are carefully considered while any changes are being planned. For example, telephone helpdesk facilities are made available for every competition, to ensure a maximum level of accessibility. A further initiative to improve both customer service and candidate accessibility was the moving of the headquarters of the Public Appointments Service to a Dublin city centre, high-street location. By establishing an actual 'Careerstore' for public service jobs, potential candidates were presented with an attractive venue that showcased the range of roles and opportunities available to public service employees. The Careerstore affords personal callers the opportunity to discuss issues with Civil Servants on a one-to-one basis, while the organisation's recruitment personnel are regularly out and about around the country making presentations and giving briefings on the latest recruitment campaigns.

The Public Appointments Service uses other technologies, with the aim of producing cost and time savings for staff, candidates and client organisations. For example, telephone conferencing is used for geographically-dispersed short-listing boards, and video interviewing is available for use with candidates in overseas locations.

Public Appointments Service staff, who shared many years of expertise in public service recruitment, played a highly significant role in establishing the new market-facing organisation. Significant levels of investment were made in training for staff in areas such as business process re-engineering (BPR), management skills, customer service and key account management. Staff throughout the organisation were encouraged to engage in the process of BPR, which resulted in many imaginative solutions focused on the needs of clients and candidates. Imagination and courage were needed to focus on what clients, taxpayers and candidates wanted, and processes were reviewed with the aim of setting increasingly higher service standards.

Culture has played a significant role in the continuing emphasis on innovation in the organisation. One hundred and fifty employees work in an inclusive and open environment, where staff are encouraged to be innovative and to contribute in whatever way they can to the organisation. The aim throughout the transformation process was to establish the Public Appointments Service as a true 'partnership organisation', where staff could be included in all significant decision-making and encouraged to participate to the fullest.

The organisation realised that a large amount of work had to be done to address the relatively low profile that public service careers had amongst key candidate groups, such as school leavers and graduates. There was a realisation that a stronger brand for public service careers needed to be communicated. The Service targeted careers fairs, organised presentations at third-level institutions, advertised in appropriate publications and addressed conferences. A lot of energy was put into making it easier for key groups to access public service campaigns. An example of this was the running of campaigns for Administrative Officer positions on university campuses around the country, thus encouraging as many graduates as possible to apply. This focus on getting the idea of civil service careers 'on the radar' resulted in an unprecedented upsurge of interest in the option of the public service as a career.

Innovation has gone to the heart of everything that the Public Appointments Service does. The organisation has begun to address the challenge of meeting the needs of a sophisticated and challenging marketplace. It is now part of the strategy of the organisation to contribute, where possible, to both the health of the wider recruitment industry and to the field of knowledge in the area of selection and human resources. In October 2004, the Public Appointments Service ran its first international conference on recruitment and selection issues, with a panel of highly-regarded international speakers. It has also established the Public Appointments Service Research Advisory Panel. Consisting of a cross section of senior public servants, academics and private sector practitioners, this panel will lead the organisation's research programme over the next number of years.

There is little complacency within the organisation, however. Employees in the Public Appointments Service realise that they offer possibly the widest range of positions in any single recruitment setting in the country and that there is a need for even greater flexibility in the future. The concept of Internet-based testing (iBT) is in an advanced state of development and will soon be rolled out as the next major recruitment and selection initiative. The speed and flexibility that iBT will afford the organisation is likely to be dramatic. In time, the Public Appointments Service see this form of testing being carried out across the Internet anywhere in the world.

The Public Appointments Service has put in place a benchmarking process that allows it to compare itself against other leading, national and international organisations. The aim of this process is to ensure that the organisation is constantly learning and changing. The ultimate judge of how well the organisation is doing will be its capacity to source the highest quality candidates for positions with client organisations.

The Public Appointments Service is now an exemplar of shared services arrangements for the civil service; a partnership arrangement with clients that delivers to clients in a way that meets their needs, and which addresses the requirements of an increasingly diverse group of candidates for the Irish public service.

8
Towards Next Practice

The cases included in this book have been identified as best practice because, in most cases, they have either been the recipient of, or have been shortlisted for, awards such as the CIPD / Watson Wyatt *National Awards for Excellence in Human Resource Management*. They are representative of courageous efforts by HR managers and chief executives to make changes to the established way of doing things in their organisational settings. It is perhaps worth reflecting on some of the characteristics of these initiatives that make them exemplars of best practice:

- Top management support was evident in all of the cases. Lip-service to an initiative is never enough by senior management in an organisation – innovative approaches to HR issues need to be sponsored and owned at the highest level in all corporate settings. The success of new practices is dependent on this.

- Each initiative is underpinned by a clearly-articulated HR strategy and plan.

- All of the approaches were responsive to the needs of the client-base of the organisation. Having the best people on board was recognised as being critical to the success of the services provided by each organisation.

- The HR managers took the needs of their employees seriously and developed tailored responses that engaged with these needs.

- The initiatives were *knowledge-based*. The teams involved took time to research and *understand* the issue and how it affected the parties involved, before developing solutions.

- There is a huge emphasis on getting the right people into the organisation and on creating environments that made them want to stay. There is a underlying ethos of 'respect' that encourages HR managers to think of staff as individual human beings, as well as sources of human and intellectual capital, which is vital to the ongoing success of the organisation.

- There is a huge awareness amongst the HR managers who provided the cases that markets, work and organisations in Irish society are undergoing fundamental change.

The challenges of today will become the norms of tomorrow and, in turn, will be replaced by a new set of issues. There is no doubt that these issues will be met 'head on' by the organisations that provided the cases for this text. It is hoped that this work will be the first in a series that will provide a continuous showcase of creative HR practices to the changes of the future.

Management and the way we think about management in general, as mentioned in the *Introduction*, is itself facing a period of fundamental change. The cases show how HR managers variously 'co-created' solutions in response to external market conditions alongside, and with, their colleagues. It is likely that future challenges will involve higher levels of participation from outside the HR function. Traditional organisational boundaries will blur and merge in the future and we are confident that some of the examples of best practice shown here will become common practice in the near future, while existing best practice firms drive the 'next practice' agenda.

It is clear that the role of the HR manager will become even more strategic, more developmental than before. In place of providing solutions to difficulties that present, HR managers will be involved in working alongside other organisational functions and employees to bring organisations to their desired futures to a much greater extent. As mentioned above, understanding the organisation and its employees is key to best practice. 'Next practice' in Human Resource Management will involve deepening this understanding and creating strong repositories of knowledge and human capital, and raising the intellectual bar for HR, to help steer organisations to their desired futures.

INDEX

Other OAK TREE PRESS titles by IMI authors

Dealing with Change: Lessons for Irish Managers
Tom McConalogue   €40 pb : ISBN 1-86076-273-5

This Management Briefing sets out to inform and educate Irish managers on the critical success factors in anticipating and managing change. The three main questions it seeks to answer are: What kind of changes are Irish organisations experiencing and how are they responding? What has helped and what has blocked Irish organisations from managing change in the past? What are some of the essential lessons for Irish companies in anticipating and managing change for the future?

Superior Customer Service: The PROMPT Approach to Success
Michael Quinn & Lynda Byron   €40 pb : ISBN 1-86076-117-8

Product quality is essential to recruiting customers, but service quality is the key to customer retention and growth. This guide presents managers with a practical approach based on a customer-centric strategy: prioritising customer needs, reliability, organising to serve customers, measures of customer satisfaction, people training, and focused technology.

The Making of Managers:
A History of the Irish Management Institute, 1952-2002
Tom Cox   €30.00 pb : ISBN 1-86076-240-9

Over the past 50 years, the Irish Management Institute (IMI) has helped to create the managers to run the changing Irish economy and has developed a reputation as one of the leading management training centres in the country. This book tells the fascinating history of the IMI, how it has made the managers and business leaders of today and the contribution it has made to Ireland's social and economic development. Today, the IMI is Ireland's centre for management development – working with individual managers and organisations to deliver results by improving the practice of management.

OAK TREE PRESS
19 Rutland Street, Cork, Ireland
T: + 353 21 431 3855   **F:** + 353 21 431 3496
E: info@oaktreepress.com
W: www.oaktreepress.com

www.oaktreepress.com

Other OAK TREE PRESS titles by IMI authors

The IMI Handbook of Management
Marion O'Connor, John Cullen & John Mangan (editors)
E60 hb : ISBN 1-86076-292-1; €40 pb : ISBN 1-86076-293-X

A 'compendium of knowledge', based on the contributors' wealth of knowledge and experience, coupled with the reputation of the IMI, makes **The IMI Handbook of Management** a uniquely relevant resource for every Irish manager – or would-be manager. The book deals with the core skills that are needed by managers to succeed in the current competitive business environment.

Contents include:

Managing Your Time	Presentation & Communication Skills
Getting Things Done	
Managing Stress & Your Health	Internal Communications
Planning Your Career	Assertiveness
Motivating Others	Influencing Others
Building Effective Teams	Gathering Business Information
Negotiating Effectively	Business Writing
Facilitating Meetings & Chairing Discussions	Managing in Changing Times
	Managing Outsourcing
Managing People	Doing Business Strategy
Managing Customers	Leadership

Each of the chapters in the **IMI Handbook of Management** is available as an eBook in PDF format (requires Adobe Acrobat Reader) from Oak Tree Press.

OAK TREE PRESS
19 Rutland Street, Cork, Ireland
T: + 353 21 431 3855 **F:** + 353 21 431 3496
E: info@oaktreepress.com
W: www.oaktreepress.com